"Practical, comprehensive and real-world. The authors are preaching what they have successfully practised for more than 15 years."
Paul McBride, CEO, Interactive Enterprise

"A very practical guide to IT Project Management with a refreshing and welcome focus on 'how to' rather than the theoretical. It is clear, comprehensive and will be a valuable tool for those engaged in managing IT projects."
Brian Healy, Director of Trading, The Irish Stock Exchange

"Up to now there had been no ready reference for the new (or old) project manager to consult at the outset of his/her new project's journey. Until now...*The No-Nonsense Project Handbook* is an easy to read, and invaluable resource – full of the obvious real world collective pain and experience of Máire and Deirdre. I can certainly see myself in those 'It could happen to you' side bars – you will too! This is a great book to have on your desk (in addition to your copy of Microsoft Project 2003 of course!)."
Clive Ryan, Business Group Lead, Information Worker, Microsoft Ireland

"With an eye towards simplicity and practicality, Máire Kearns and Deirdre Fox provide a powerhouse of tips, templates and checklists to bring even the most challenging project under control. In a nutshell, *The No-Nonsense Project Handbook* provides everything you need to know about successfully managing any project."
Joe Nedder, CEO SofCheck, Inc

"This is a pragmatic and practical handbook for anyone who has to deliver IT projects. It is full of real world experience, including useful templates and checklists by two seasoned project managers who have embraced the many challenges we face in IT project delivery."
Martin Downes, Vice President, Enterprise, Trintech Technologies

"This practical guide to IT Project Management walks the reader, step-by-step, through every stage of the project life cycle, clearly defining roles, responsibilities and deliverables. Each chapter is self-contained so it works equally well as a training guide and/or as a reference manual. We have incorporated many of the ideas presented in this book into our Project Life Cycle methodology and this has helped to improve the overall quality of our projects."
Ronan Swan, Senior Information Systems Manager, Xilinx

About the Authors

Authors photograph © Orla O'Brien

MÁIRE KEARNS and DEIRDRE FOX have worked in the IT industry since 1990. They currently run a very successful consulting and training company (Blue Sky Training and Consulting), advising multinational clients on project delivery and management. Prior to this they both worked as senior operational directors of a large US consultancy firm. They have worked with multinational companies in the US, Europe and Ireland implementing complex strategic projects. Using their project management technique, all of their projects have been completed on time and within budget.

Over the years they have harvested their knowledge and developed significant training and mentorship programmes, training both clients and employees in project management arenas. They have spoken at numerous conferences and seminars, and written articles for various trade magazines. They are members of the Institute of Business Analysis and Consulting.

OM.

LEABHARLANNA CHONTAE NA GAILLIMHE
(GALWAY COUNTY LIBRARIES)

Acc. No....H 154055.... Class No......658-022

Date of Return	Date of Return	Date of Return

ORANMORE LIBRARY

Books are on loan for 21 days from date of issue.

Fines for overdue books: 10c for each week or portion of a week plus cost of postage incurred in recovery.

Testimonials – The No-Nonsense Project Handbook

"Máire Kearns and Deirdre Fox are two of the most experienced Project Delivery experts in the software industry, having delivered projects for major corporations around the world on time and on budget. This book, at last, describes in a concise, usable format the entire successful project management and delivery process, and is an indispensable guide for every project manager and technology executive. It is mandatory in our organization and should be in every technologists bookshelf. Finally, a book written by people who have been there and done it successfully."

Paraic O'Toole, CEO, Automsoft

"This is an essential book for both seasoned and beginner Project Managers. The book is full of practical hints that are very easy to understand and that reflect real life. A must read for all project managers."

Padraic Mills, Director of IT, Administration and Innovation, AXA Ireland

"This book takes a pragmatic and simple approach to breaking down the critical components of the planning, execution and measurement of a successful project. So many Project Management books and approaches espouse the use of abstract methodologies, GANTT charts and waterfall diagrams where the desire of the project owner, particularly those less experienced, is to have a clear understanding of the more common issues that happen in the trenches. This is the sort of resource I would have loved to have had 7–8 years ago, I am sure it would have made me a more effective manager and would have been a significant benefit to our company's performance and success."

Michael Galvin, General Manager, Cisco Systems Internetworking (Ireland) Ltd

"At last! A plain-speaking, straight-talking guide for IT Project Managers that they can use and reuse every day on real-world projects. A good complement to the more formal project management books."

Dr Sanjiv Gossain, Vice President, Cognizant Technology Solutions

"In this book, Deirdre Fox and Máire Kearns clarify the challenges for successfully delivering IT projects, a problem that faces all organisations. Their unique approach is practical and concise, and is based upon invaluable real world expertise. If you are involved in IT projects, I recommend that you reference this book on a frequent basis."

Dr Chris Horn, Vice Chairman, Iona Technologies

The No-Nonsense Project Handbook

GALWAY COUNTY LIBRARIES

FOX and KEARNS

BLACKHALL
PUBLISHING

This book was typeset by

ASHFIELD PRESS PUBLISHING SERVICES

for

BLACKHALL PUBLISHING
33 Carysfort Avenue
Blackrock
Co. Dublin
Ireland

e-mail: info@blackhallpublishing.com
www.blackhallpublishing.com

© Fox and Kearns, 2005

ISBN: 1 842180 89 4

A catalogue record for this book is available from the British Library.

Printed in Ireland by
ColourBooks Ltd

For Niall and Ronan

Acknowledgements

We would like to thank all the following people who gave their time and thoughts in helping us produce this book. Thank you especially to all our clients world-wide, who allowed us to learn and gain invaluable experience while working on their projects. To all of our great colleagues who even during the craziest projects always made sure we had fun! To Caitríona Diviney and Stephen and Gillian Mulligan, who had to suffer the first draft and advised on many improvements. Thank you to Jeremy Graham for his advice, which as usual he delivered on time!

Sincere thanks to Maria Battaglia, Gina and John Eddison, Mary Hope, David Mulligan, Fergal Mullen, Fionnáin O'Dwyer and Ray Noone for all their valuable input.

And as always a really special thanks goes to our fabulous support team: Chris and Willie; Nancy and Frank; Vera and Seán; and Nuala and Joe. And also to Nuala Hannon, Loreto Farrell, Susan Mulligan and Siobhán Swan, who never seem to say "no"!

Thank you to Gerard, Ruth and Susan of Blackhall Publishing for guiding us each and every step of the way.

And if you are reading this now, we thank you too and wish you every success with all your projects!

Contents

Chapter 12: Testing

Chapter 13: Project planning and estimation

Besides the noble art of getting things done, there is the noble art of leaving things undone ... The wisdom of life consists in the elimination of nonessentials.

- Lin Yutang, Chinese writer and educator.

CHAPTER 1

Introduction

*Help – I've to deliver an IT project! Where do I start, what do I do, who do
I need, what don't I know, how can I get out of this project?*

We have heard those cries a million times. In fact we have been
where you are now! We have been handed a project and told to
deliver it by a certain "impossible" date. We have done the 24-hour
shifts, we have had team members taken from us during critical
phases, we have worked with the users who keep changing their
minds, we have had the developers who forgot to back up, we have
had the external consultants who haven't delivered on their promises, we have had budgets cut and above all we have had the constant
mental torment! We know how hard IT projects can be! With over
fifteen years' experience though we can now definitively say what
works and what does not. We have harvested all our knowledge and
experiences into a set of very successful consultative training
programmes for clients worldwide and now we have decided to pass
the information on further by writing this book. It was actually our
clients that suggested we write it!

This book is written for anyone who has to run any aspect of an
IT project, whether you are a consultant working for external
customers or are part of an IT department working for internal
customers. It is not a theoretical book; it is a practical book focusing
on what will get you through the everyday life of the unpredictable
IT project.

People tend to evolve into the role of project manager (PM),
usually coming from a development background or some other
management discipline. We find that PMs can typically be divided
into three types of people: those who are technically sound with
zero to little management skills, those who have some management
skills with zero to little knowledge of IT and those who have
neither!

And these PMs never get real-world project delivery training. Their training (if any) is typically theoretical, high level and not relevant to the everyday life of an IT project, and it is often delivered by a lecturer who has never lived the ups and downs of delivering an IT project. And let's face it, IT projects are different; they have their own culture and their own bad reputations. We know, we have lived it!

Who should Read this Book?

The No-Nonsense Project Handbook is aimed at anyone who is involved in delivering IT projects, i.e. PMs, technical leaders (TLs), developers, business managers and users. We wrote it with a few audiences in mind. We felt that firstly *PMs* need a simply laid-out handbook outlining, step by step, the daily tasks for each phase of a project that they could refer to on a daily basis. We felt that PMs should be able to hand this book to all their team members and show them how their project will be run! We wrote it for *TLs* who need to manage and keep on top of the technical solution and who will find the detailed technical checklists beneficial. For the advanced technical reader please note that this book is focusing on managing IT projects and needs to be supplemented with technical manuals and references for in-depth technical information on technical areas such as architecture, hardware, databases, networks, infrastructures etc. We wrote it for *developers* who very often are just given code to write and are rarely included in the overall big picture of a project. We also felt that young developers still in or just graduated from college can learn very valuable professional lessons from this book. We often found that graduates just out of college had no idea how to blend into IT projects, i.e. what they should do and what they should not do! They will also benefit from all the technical checklists. We wrote it for *business managers* who may hail from finance, HR, marketing, sales etc., letting them know what is expected of them. The top reason why IT projects fail of course is the lack of user involvement. So we also wrote this book for users who are constantly frustrated by not getting the requirements they asked for, are often slightly in fear of IT people and baffled as to how projects actually get implemented. We wrote it for *the user* who wants to know how IT projects should be run, what role they should be playing and how to define their requirements in a comprehensible manner. There are many useful checklists and recommendations for the user who has to interact with IT projects, departments or people.

Very often the issue for someone managing an IT project is that they don't even know what questions to ask. This book will be your coach and turn you into a competent PM over a weekend!

The Objective of this Book

We feel that you should be able to read this book over a weekend or a long-haul flight! The purpose of this book is to hand-hold you through an entire IT project lifecycle, i.e. from initiation to rollout. We have:

❑ Defined the roles and responsibilities for team members
❑ Defined how to manage your team and your customer
❑ Shown you how to best manage the delivery of the project from start to finish
❑ Provided best-practice guides for gathering requirements, estimating and project planning
❑ Explained how to run efficient workshops and requirement-gathering sessions
❑ Included project justification checklists
❑ Provided developer checklists, for example coding standards, unit tests, code reviews etc.
❑ Presented an innovative comprehensive guide on best practices for managing the testing phases, i.e. system test, user acceptance test (UAT) etc.

We feel sure that after reading this book you will feel confident in knowing what you need to know about running an IT project as well as what you do not need to know – which is just as important!

Style of the Chapters

We have purposely kept the style of this book simple. You should be able to read each chapter independently and gather your information, as you need it. You will notice that each chapter has a similar format and includes:

❑ A "Thought provoker" at the start – just to get you thinking

- ❏ An "In a nutshell" definition of the topic to be discussed
- ❏ A detailed description of the topic
- ❏ "Tip" and "Warning" boxes that highlight key tips or items to remember and watch out for
- ❏ An "It could happen to you" story that shows you the odd things that have happened to us and could happen to you and hopefully makes you realise that your project is actually normal!
- ❏ Templates and checklists.

Conclusion

We have refined and used this methodology across all our projects worldwide. IT works! When used properly, you can be sure your project will come in on time and on budget. You can also be pretty sure that you can enjoy a life outside of work. We hope you find it helpful and wish you every success with any project you may be planning for the future. Please contact us if you have any questions or suggestions through info@blueskytraining.ie

CHAPTER 2

The Project Manager

"PM's should never be afraid to say 'no' and should always feel comfortable saying 'I don't know'."

The PM in a Nutshell

The role of the PM can vary across organisations. However, to run an IT project properly the PM role should be very clearly defined and understood. The PM is responsible for the overall integrity of a project, the delivery of a project on time and within budget and the quality of all deliverables. The PM develops the project plan and ensures milestones and cost objectives are met. They are responsible for the day-to-day management of the complete project team, i.e. the delivery team and customer team. It is important to remember that if you are a PM you "should" not be responsible for the mistakes of others, but you "will be" considered responsible!

The PM sets the tone of a project; a dull and dreary PM will inevitably mean a dull and dreary project! Project managers should be dynamic, knowledgeable (about all aspects of a project), mentors, strong-willed, forthright, good negotiators, fair and firm, and above all enjoy a sense of team fun. A good PM will recognise that there is life outside of running a project too and manage accordingly!

So what are the goals of a PM? The key goals are listed below:

The Goals of a PM

- ☑ To meet the agreed project requirements.
- ☑ To fulfil the project contract within the required time and cost.
- ☑ To demonstrate that the business benefits will be achieved and where possible manage that achievement.

✓ To manage customer expectations to a level that the project meets or exceeds them.
✓ To ensure the highest possible level of customer satisfaction.
✓ To remain responsive to the customer needs throughout the whole project.
✓ To manage the project team.

The Responsibilities of a PM

This is the IT PM's job description. Yes there is a lot to do, but if you do it all you will succeed!

Responsibilities	
Manage the work	❑ Plan, organise, control and lead the project. ❑ Prepare project and team schedules. ❑ Define staffing requirements. ❑ Prepare contracts. ❑ Define the project plan. ❑ Estimate and define time-frames, complexity and costs for the project. ❑ Manage the project operations and logistics (e.g. booking rooms, lunch etc.). ❑ Delegate activities and tasks. ❑ Monitor, maintain and update the schedule as the project progresses. ❑ Understand the functionality of the application. ❑ Understand the business impact of the application. ❑ Identify "scope creep". ❑ Test the application. ❑ Monitor the issues, risks and assumptions . ❑ Monitor the quality of the project, ensuring deliverables are of a high quality.
Manage the costs	❑ Estimate the cost. ❑ Monitor and update the project costing spreadsheet. ❑ Update the business case through the scope and design phases.

Manage the people – executives, management, team, business users, other IT staff, vendors	❑ Build relationships with the executives, the business users and other IT staff. ❑ Manage expectations about the project. ❑ Assign team roles and responsibilities. ❑ Mentor team members. ❑ Coordinate team meetings and customer meetings. ❑ Coordinate checkpoints. ❑ Manage the test phases, i.e. system, user, production. ❑ Provide weekly status updates to the delivery and customer teams. ❑ Manage team dynamics and ensure the team is working together effectively. ❑ Maintain team morale. ❑ Complete project reviews for each member of the delivery team. ❑ Organise sunset reviews (i.e. review of project post implementation). ❑ Manage scope creep.

Warning: A PM should avoid "cost" discussions with customers where possible. While a PM must be fully aware of cost implications for a project, ideally they should be seen purely in an operational role. Where possible an account manager, a project sponsor or a business manager should handle cost negotiations for the PM.

So Good PMs ...

✓ Take control of a project and enforce the project methodology.

✓ Are very efficient and organised, and always deliver on promises – no matter how small.

✓ Are tuned in and prepared to admit when they're baffled!

✓ Do not hide from the customer and are not bullied by the customer. This is achieved by being meticulous about documentation and constantly documenting agreements, issue resolutions and assumptions.

✓ Are totally focused and clearly know the end solution, i.e. what's *in* and what's *not in*.

✓ Demand that users, customers and executives follow

project processes and procedures and protect their team.
- ✓ Can say *no* and stick to it!
- ✓ Can negotiate and do not over-promise out of fear!
- ✓ Are liked by customers because of honesty and seem to be fair.
- ✓ Are prepared to listen to the team and take a chance, i.e. are always focusing on the 80/20 rule and searching for a little bit of the "Wow" factor.
- ✓ Know what they need to know and what they don't need to know, what they need to do and what they don't need to do!

The PM Skill Set

Hard Skills	Soft Skills
❑ Project management	❑ Presentation
❑ General management (plan, lead, organise, control)	❑ Communication
❑ IT	❑ Negotiation
❑ Accounting and finance	❑ Problem solving
❑ Marketing	❑ Decision making
❑ Operations management	❑ Assertiveness
❑ Strategic management	❑ Influencing and motivation
❑ Consultancy	❑ Stress management
❑ Human resource (HR) management	❑ Emotional resilience
❑ Leadership	

The PM Responsibilities, Phase by Phase, throughout the Project Lifecycle

The following table is a sample of the type of PM responsibilities during the different phases of a project lifecycle. At the start of a project it is very useful to give this to a team showing them what role the PM will play on the project. Use it as part of the norming session (see Chapter 3). Human resources can also use this when they have to hire a PM, as often the complete PM skill set is misunderstood. This table can be modified to suit individual needs.

Phase	Responsibilities
Scope	❏ Coordinate team to meet deliverables. ❏ Build relationships with account managers, executives, project sponsors, users etc. ❏ Build relationship with the customer. ❏ Manage customer expectations. ❏ Work with the customer to build schedules and identify people requirements. ❏ Assign team roles and responsibilities. ❏ Work on time and price estimates for future phases (see below). ❏ Manage the overall operations and logistics of the scope. ❏ Coordinate project staffing. ❏ Manage the delivery of a quality scope document. ❏ Manage the delivery of a quality scope presentation. ❏ Manage customer sign-off.
Design	❏ Guide, supervise and set expectations with team members. ❏ Maintain/update design schedule. ❏ Maintain team morale. ❏ Understand the high-level functionality of the application. ❏ Coordinate team meetings. ❏ Coordinate staffing. ❏ Coordinate participation of customer, user and technical staff. ❏ Provide status to internal management and customer management. ❏ Manage team dynamics and ensure team works effectively together. ❏ Update outside groups weekly if applicable (e.g. senior technical specialists). ❏ Estimate complexity and duration of tasks for development. ❏ Complete development project plan. ❏ Manage the delivery of a quality design document. ❏ Manage customer sign-off.
Development	❏ Ensure project is on schedule (both from a time and cost perspective) and deliverables meet quality standards.

	❑ Coordinate Quality Assurance (QA) review.
	❑ Monitor and track project's progress.
	❑ Organise change implementation plans.
	❑ Understand the high-level functionality of the application.
	❑ Understand the functionality in the current phase and identify and manage scope.
	❑ Guide, supervise and set expectations with team members.
	❑ Assign tasks and modules for development.
	❑ Manage team dynamics and ensure team works effectively together.
	❑ Organise team events (delivery and customer teams)
	❑ Maintain team morale.
	❑ Identify and understand integration points.
	❑ Manage the assimilation of the project application with the user and business and technical teams.
	❑ Coordinate team meetings.
	❑ Coordinate major checkpoints.
	❑ Build test plans.
	❑ Manage and approve system test, user and production acceptance testing.
	❑ Coordinate participation of user and technical teams
	❑ Coordinate staffing.
	❑ Ensure contractual obligations are met and help resolve any issues.
	❑ Main customer liaison – manage customer expectations, deliverables and issues.
	❑ Advocate of the team and representative for the team.
	❑ Manage and supervise implementation of any change/process management procedures.
	❑ Review and approve project documentation.
Project wrap-up	❑ Review all team members on a formal basis.
	❑ Organise sunset and quality reviews.
	❑ Harvest project information and ensure "Lessons Learned" are fed back into the organisation.
	❑ Harvest reusable components from project.
	❑ Update project documentation and methodology guidelines if necessary.
	❑ Present sunset review presentation to other teams, management, users etc.
	❑ Organise sunset review with customer.

Pricing and Monitoring Project Costs

The two typical options for costing your project are:

1. Fixed Time Fixed Price: The delivery date and cost are agreed per phase. An estimate is provided for any outstanding phases. Where possible avoid providing a fixed time and price for the entire project before the design phase. You will not have enough information!
2. Time and Materials (T&M): The project cost if based upon team requirements, duration and expenses. Typically weekly time sheets outlining hours and costs are submitted to the customer. If you have a choice you should select this option!

When pricing your project you need to keep the following costs in mind. As a PM, you will need to monitor costs throughout the lifecycle of the project to ensure you are within the original budget.

Sample Project Costs

Resources	Daily Rate per Resource
Expenses	Air travel (agree "fly back" policy, e.g. every second weekend) Other travel Car rental Food and lodgings Entertainment Equipment rental Training Team events Taxis Per diems Administration (printing, photocopying, manuals etc.)
Hardware/Hosting	Servers PCs Support Printers etc.
Software	Product Licensing fees Support etc.
Human Resource	Hiring and recruitment
Consultants	External consultants

It Could Happen to you ...

The Very Agreeable PM

I worked for a PM that did not understand how to say no to a customer – it was a nightmare! There was a team of ten people working on a project that was fixed time and fixed price, and was due to be delivered within a really tight schedule. Everyone was working tough hours anyway, but each day the customer would take the PM into a room and provide him with a change request (not even an official change request!). The customer would play it as "just a little change" and the PM would agree to it without ever discussing it or its impact with the team. This of course put tremendous strain on the team, from a delivery perspective but even more so from a team morale perspective. The team ultimately had no respect for the PM and everyone wanted to get off the project as quickly as possible.

This PM was foolish. A very detailed design document had been signed-off by the customer. Each change should have been compared to the design document and an "official" change request should have been created for each change. Each request should then have been estimated from both a time and cost perspective and that would have made the customer PM re-think many of those changes. His budget and/or deadline would have been changed and this would have made him think long and hard before signing off the change. Unfortunately for our poor team the customer just demanded and demanded, and got what he wanted, as he knew our PM was too weak to say no.

CHAPTER 3

Team Management

> "I know you think you know what you thought I meant but I don't think you really know what I know I meant."

The Team in a Nutshell

When a project gets approval, the first step for a PM is to gather and inform a team of people about it. The team will consist of full-time and part-time roles, each with their own defined set of deliverables for each phase of the project. As the PM you need to know what skill sets are required, when and for how long. You will also need to be very prompt in informing your customer of their team requirements and their time commitments. The trickiest aspect for you with the start of every project is getting your team operational as quickly and as smoothly as possible. The PM must be seen to be a very confident leader and very confident in knowing how to get the project delivered. You must enforce the methodology and norms for a successful project and you must set out clearly defined processes, roles and responsibilities for each team member. When you get your team together you need to focus on the following:

❏ Defining your team structure
❏ Jump-starting your team
❏ Defining your team "must dos".

Defining your Team Structure

A project team can range from 2 to 222 people! No matter what size team you have you need to apply the same project principles to that team. Decide what the project deliverables are and who you will need to get them done.

The following is a typical IT project team structure:

Figure 3.1: **Typical IT Team Structure**

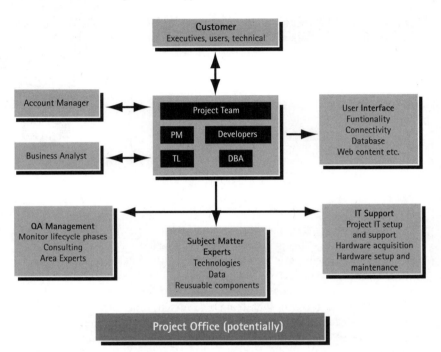

TL – Technical Leader
PM – Project Manager
DBA – Database Analyst

When implementing an IT project you will need expertise at some stage during the project from most of the roles listed above. How much time you need from each will depend upon the project type, duration, budget and priority. Refer to the chapters on scope (9), design (10), development (11) and testing (12) for further definition of team requirements.

A Note on the Project Office (PO)

The Project Office (PO) is an environment that is set up to manage large-scale projects or multiple smaller projects within the one organisation. POs should certainly be set up when an organisation has multiple locations and is aiming to standardise technologies, methodologies, release procedures, testing standards etc. across all locations.

The term *programme* is used to refer to the complete set of individual projects. The PO is generally staffed with a cross-functional team that consists of senior operational people, i.e. a programme manager, technical architect, business manager, QA manager, IT managers and a core group of super users who together have the responsibility to manage the overall scope, vision, technical direction and quality of all the individual projects. Project managers usually report into the programme manager.

Programme management is fundamentally different from project management in several ways:

❏ Programme managers need to be "managers of managers": coaches, mentors, confidants, trusted advisors and leaders

❏ Programme managers need to coordinate and manage the multiple, concurrent projects that make up the programme; they have to focus on interdependency and "The Big Picture"

❏ Programme managers need to worry about moves to production, ongoing operation and support issues, scheduling multiple projects, managing multiple teams and the overall strategic direction of the whole organisation.

If you Have to Develop a Programme Plan

Before beginning individual project phases on a large programme, it is critical that a programme planning session be held with all appropriate parties responsible for delivering tasks critical to the overall success of the programme. The programme plan has implications outside the responsibilities of each individual project team, i.e. operations, business, training, organisational, external suppliers etc. The output of this session is a comprehensive programme plan which is different to a project plan in that it:

☑ Is constructed at a higher level
☑ Encompasses multiple projects, potentially across multiple locations
☑ Involves several responsible parties including external suppliers

Is coordination oriented, rather than task oriented.

To be effective, programme plans must be based upon milestones and dependencies developed by the PO team, PMs and customer representatives.

The PO essentially allows individual PMs to concentrate on project-specific delivery issues, so they don't have to worry about high-level coordination, integration and strategic-level management tasks. It allows the PM the time to deliver their own specific project on time, knowing the PO is managing the other interdependent projects.

Jump-Starting your Team

To get your team up and running as quickly as possible we recommend that you organise a formal "Norming" session.

What is Norming?

Dr Bruce Tuckman published his Forming, Storming, Norming, Performing model in 1965.* In a subsequent 1977 article, "Stages of Small-Group Development Revisited"**, Tuckman and coauthor Mary Ann Jensen noted that subsequent studies suggested a termination stage which they named adjourning.

The forming, storming, norming, performing theory is a helpful explanation of team dynamics and group behaviour. It is important that a PM understand this. We like to summarise it as follows:

Forming: When a team gets together there is an initial orientation stage of getting to know each other, figuring out their role and position in the group, testing each other's capabilities and skills. There tends to be little agreement on team direction other than what is presented by the PM.

Storming: At this stage team members try to establish themselves in relation to the team and the leader. They may even challenge each other, which may lead to power struggles and the formation of cliques. The team is in an unproductive state of discontent.

---

*   Tuckman, Bruce W. (1965) Developmental Sequence in Small Groups. Copyright 1965 by the American Psychological Association.
** *Psychological Bulletin*, Vol. 63, No. 6, pp. 384–99.

Norming: During this stage agreement and consensus on roles and responsibilities is formed amongst the team, who begin to respond well to leadership by the PM. The team develops its own processes and style of working. There is general respect for the PM and some of the leadership responsibilities are divided out amongst the team.

Performing: The team now clearly knows its purpose and is actually performing and producing results. The team is able to work towards achieving a goal and there is a sense of camaraderie amongst team members.

Adjourning: This is the break-up stage of the team. Management should be sensitive to people's vulnerabilities in this stage. Team members tend to feel a sense of insecurity when their team is disbanded, especially if they have been closely bonded during the project.

How to Run a Norming Session

To avoid wasting time, emotions and effort and possible irreparable morale damage on the forming and storming phases we recommend that you jump-start to a formal norming session to get the team operational as soon as possible.

Norming is an absolute must at the start of every project phase. You should arrange it during preparation time. Make sure you get everyone who will be involved in the project at some stage in a room together for about three hours. People who cannot physically be present should conference in. As PM you will need to prepare a lot of background material for a norming session and you can get some of the team to help out. The objective at the end of a norming session is to ensure team consensus on the project deliverables and goals, the project methodology, roles and responsibilities, methods of working together and agreed actions. Here is a sample norming agenda:

Sample Norming Agenda
Explain what norming is.

Introductions from each person stating:
    ❑ Name and past project experience
    ❑ How they like to work and what they don't like
    ❑ Their personal expectations for the project.

Assignment of roles and responsibilities.
Project overview: plan, deliverables, time-frames.

Customer background:
   ❑ Who's who?
   ❑ Their areas of pain; their requirements
   ❑ Project background and documentation to date
   ❑ Any other ongoing projects that may have an impact.

Project methodology.
Project tools.
Project standards: documentation, coding etc.
Project environment.
Project deliverables.
Project issues and assumptions.
Team concerns/worries.

Project administration:
   ❑ Housekeeping: documentation, meetings, holiday requests,
      finance (expenses, taxis, per diems, training)
   ❑ Documentation: non-disclosure agreements (NDAs), vendor
      agreements, statements of work, contracts etc.

PM expectations: ground rules, standards, interpersonal behaviour.
Questions and answers.
Generation of action list.

Tip: While norming may seem like common sense it is amazing how often it is neglected at the start of projects. "Unnormed" teams usually have serious communication problems and misunderstandings about the overall project. If a project team is showing these symptoms, take time out to "re-norm" them.

Some Common Ground Rules

The following are just sample ground rules that are usually agreed during a norming session. It is often a lack of agreement of these simple rules that causes team conflict later on!

Ground Rules	
Work hours e.g. "The core hours are 10:00 a.m. – 4:30 p.m." All team members must be available during these hours; after that it is up to individual team members how they want to manage their work.	**Travel e.g.** "Overseas team members can fly home every weekend." This may even mean a team member has to leave early on Friday evenings.

Communication e.g. "The PM is the prime contact with customer." Any requirements or changes with the customer must be run by PM.	**Team meetings/checkpoints e.g.** "Team meeting every Monday morning at 9:30 a.m." All team members must attend (or phone in) and have a status report ready.
Holidays/vacations e.g. "Four weeks' notice required for any vacation arrangements." All team members should notify the PM of vacation plans at the norming session.	**Music e.g.** "Headsets must be used." This particularly applies to development teams who like to write code while listening to music, as this can be disruptive for those who don't!
Work environment e.g. "Desks are hot desks." Team cannot get possessive about their chairs, staplers, phones etc. They are for general use.	**Confidentiality e.g.** "The project is confidential." Team must know if they cannot talk openly about the project. They should be given a standard statement about the project.
Mobile phones e.g. "Mobile phones on silent." There is nothing more annoying than the constant hum of ring tones in a development area!	**Team romance rule e.g.** "No team or customer romance." It can be uncomfortable. Try to hold off until the project is over or hide it well!

Some Notes on the Session

- ❏ A person who is not directly involved in the project should facilitate the norming session.
- ❏ Norming meeting notes must be documented and distributed to every team member afterwards.
- ❏ As PM you should ensure that there is consensus amongst the team when the session has ended.

Running a Project – Some Rules of Engagement

When running a project it is imperative that team members know exactly how to behave with their own team members and in front of the customer. A PM or customer should not be shocked by a team member! The following are some basic rules of behaviour when on a project team.

Rule	Description
Never agree anything with the customer unless the PM is involved	A good PM is totally clear on the scope of the project and is very focused on what is in and out. Besides the TL, few others tend to be as clear. It is therefore imperative that team members do not agree to deliver anything without approval of the PM. Your full team must be aware of this. Customers will try to sneak in requirements through other channels!
Never estimate on the fly	Sometimes during requirements meetings eager team members can start estimating requirements on the spot, thinking that something might be simple. Even if it seems simple, keep quiet until the full team has had time to review and estimate the requirement.
Never have bright ideas in front of the customer!	Discuss any new ideas with the PM first! Certainly be creative but keep your creativity to yourself until you have had time to estimate it. Once customers hear it they tend to want it and it may be out of scope!
Avoid confrontation in front of the customer	Sessions can get heated (they should if you are running a good project!). Different people in a room can have very different ideas. However, never disagree with your own team members openly. Save it until later. Dissent on a project team is unprofessional.
Never be aggressive with a customer	If the scope of the project is creeping you must remain firm but professional; there is always a middle ground. Do not prolong a disagreement and use timeouts to resolve issues. Never lose your head – you will lose all respect!
Document everything and provide feedback to the customer	Document after every interaction with the customer. Use your issues and assumptions log or your requirement matrix. These will usually be affected! Review all updates with the customer at the weekly status meeting.
Allow sufficient customer reading time for all deliverables	This is often forgotten! When creating a project plan allow one to two days at the end of each deliverable to allow the customer time to read and review the document. Plan for a feedback session too.

All team members should expect to facilitate customer sessions	It is good for the team and good for the PM to rotate the facilitation of customer sessions. No one is exempt. Prepare the agenda well and stick to the rules of workshops (see Chapter 4).
Plan for social events	For large projects it is important to allow for team events and a bit of fun; plan for it in your project budget. It will help the general interaction with all team members.
Never lose formality with your customer	The number of times we see this one ignored! We have seen junior developers chat up the executive sponsor's wife. What can we say? There's nothing worse – just don't do it!

Your Team Must Dos

1. Hold weekly team meetings. ✓
2. Hold weekly customer meetings and manage the customer. ✓
3. Manage issues, risks and assumptions. ✓
4. Revise your project plan. ✓

There are two fundamental golden rules for running any IT project:

1. Always organise a short weekly delivery team status meeting
2. Always organise a short weekly customer team status meeting.

With these two meetings alone you will be sure to keep your project on track. Projects can get into difficulty through lack of diligence in holding these meetings. We have actually seen PMs avoid them because they don't want the hassle! These two meetings alone will help mitigate problems that typically cause project failure.

Having reviewed numerous projects on a worldwide basis the following issues always float to the top:

The Most Common Project Issues
Lack of status reports and communication, i.e. lack of weekly/daily customer and team meetings.
Poor documentation, i.e. not done daily and to quality standard.

Lack of attention to detail, i.e. poor requirements definition, capturing and documentation.
Team did not raise issues, i.e. they had no opportunity to do so.
Poor issues and assumptions management, i.e. the issues and assumptions log was not monitored.
Poor scope management, i.e. poor documentation, no sign-off, no expectation setting and weak project management.
Team lack of knowledge and understanding about original deliverable, i.e. no norming session, lack of weekly meetings.
Customer did not know project expectations and methodology, i.e. customer was not educated on the project process, lack of weekly meetings.
External vendors did not meet deadlines, i.e. external vendors were not managed, educated or embarrassed(!) on project milestones.

1. Hold Weekly Team Meetings

These can be short and snappy but with a focus on detail. The full team should attend or conference in.

- ❑ Suggest every Monday morning at the same time
- ❑ Meetings should last one hour maximum
- ❑ Agenda:
  - – PM update
  - – Status from each team member
  - – Revised "To Do" list
- ❑ Review issues, risks and assumptions log
- ❑ Enforce a late arrival penalty
- ❑ Follow up with a simple team checkpoint report.

2. Hold Weekly Customer Meetings and Manage the Customer

Before you start the project tell your customer how you work. Give them a short presentation on the lifecycle of the project and present to them on a formal basis your project plan, any planned milestones, checkpoints and your expectation for their attendance at the weekly meetings. Get them to present to you a similar presentation so both teams understand each other.

Remember, your customer has expected roles and responsibilities too that must be made clear to them upfront. Some include:

Customer Responsibilities
Providing appropriate user, technical and executive personnel.
Providing workspace and technical environment for work performed at their site.
Working with the development team to ensure that the technical environment outlined is in place to support the schedule.
Ensuring consulting support is available to the development team.
Defining general business rules, escalation rules etc.
Resolving critical business issues on a timely basis.
Empowering their subject matter experts to have authority to make design decisions for the project.
Managing any other external parties involved in the project.
Ensuring end-user groups are available and capable of participating in all phases.
Reviewing and signing-off relevant documentation.
Creating and documenting test scenarios.
Attending weekly status meetings.

The Customer Weekly Status Meeting

❑ Suggest every Friday morning at the same time.

❑ Meetings should last one hour maximum.

❑ PM should send the status report (traffic light report – see below) to the customer PM for review on Thursday night.

❑ Attendees: the delivery team (PM, TL, account manager/business manager) and the customer team (PM and all interested customer parties, i.e. users, sponsor, IT, business and other vendors).

❑ Agenda:
  – PM update – traffic light report (see below)
  – Status from customer
  – "To Dos" for both teams
  – Review issues, risks and assumptions log.

A Note on Customer Issue Resolution

When a serious issue arises you need to manage the situation immediately.

✓ Meet with the customer and get all their issues on a flipchart – don't get defensive, let them vent all their issues first.

✓ Do not meet the customer alone bring someone along to document.

✓ See what issues you can work through – some may be just clarifications.

- ☑ Park ones you do not want to/cannot handle – but promise the customer a meeting with your manager to work through these.
- ☑ Make an action list.
- ☑ Prepare your manager immediately by sending them your meeting notes.
- ☑ Arrange a meeting with your manager and the customer to resolve the rest of the issues.
- ☑ Document all agreements and promises made and distribute.
- ☑ Continue weekly customer meetings.

Sample Weekly Status Report/Traffic Light Report

Date:

Attendees:

Actions this week

No.	Description

Status Summary

Red
❑
❑
❑

Orange
❑
❑
❑

Green
❑
❑
❑

Issues

No.	Description	Date Raised	Raised by	Assigned to/ Resolved by	Status

Assumptions

No.	Assumption	Date Raised

Risk Register

No.	Risk	Probability Rating (PR) 1–5	Impact Rating (IR) 1–5	Exposure (PR X IR)	Mitigation Plan

A Note on the Traffic Light Report

It is crucial that this report gets updated on a weekly basis. We have seen customers design overly complicated status reports and then complain that they do not get completed! Your status report must capture the critical information that tracks the status of your project, which this one does. More importantly, however, you should constantly review the issues and assumptions log and you must ensure that your customers read and sign them off weekly.

3. Manage Issues, Risks and Assumptions

Issues, risks and assumptions are inseparable. Try not to get caught up on risk calculations and the difference between issues and risks. Some believe that serious mathematical calculations and spreadsheets are required to assess and calculate risk. Maybe so for some projects, but most IT projects just need a risk or issue register that warns the team of impending trouble using critical, high, medium or low ratings.

What Is the Difference between Risks and Issues?

❏   Issues are absolute – they will happen; risks are probable – they may or may not happen.

❏   An issue is something that has happened, is happening or is about to happen; a risk is something that may happen at some point in time.

❏   A risk that is not successfully mitigated or deflected may become more and more certain until it becomes an issue; at this point the impact is certain unless you resolve it very quickly.

❏   Assumptions are factors that, for planning purposes, will be considered to be true, real or certain. Assumptions generally carry a degree of risk – the risk that the assumption will not turn out to be true, real or certain – and are managed in the same way as risks. For example: "It is assumed that the customer IT team will have the complete test environment (as outlined in the design document) set up and ready by 1 October – Start of System Test Phase."

4. Revise your Project Plan

Project managers often neglect to add time into their project plan for managing the development team and the customer. The following should be given "time" considerations when creating the initial project plan:

❏   Team management – training, norming, documentation

❏   Team meetings – when, where, how often, how long?

❏   Customer management – training, customer responsibilities, issue resolution

❏   Customer meetings – who, when, where, how often, how long?

❏   Formal checkpoint presentations (usually every two months) – who, when, where, how often, how long?

❏   Internal management – status reports (when and how often?), operations meetings (should be weekly), QA reviews, for example code reviews, reuse reviews etc.

It Could Happen to you ...

The Not-So-Mobile PM!

An IT project lends itself very easily to working in an open plan office environment. Upon visiting a team one day for a quality review, I noticed a very tense atmosphere amongst the developers and upon further probing this anger was unified against the PM. Apparently, and I quote, "the PM hadn't grasped the concept yet of the mobile phone", the concept being that he could bring it around with him! When he was not at his desk he left his mobile phone there. His mobile rang a loud very annoying ring tone, which decimated a very concentrated environment. Of course, when he didn't answer the phone they all then had to listen to the more annoying "message received" ring tone! After many attempts to inform him of the annoyance the team eventually took measures into their own hands. One day the PM could not find his phone; only after many hours of searching did he eventually discover it stuck in a potted plant sitting outside on the windowsill of the fifth floor!

CHAPTER 4

Running Workshops

"Consensus does not mean that everyone thinks that the best decision was made or even that they are sure it will work – what it does mean is that everyone had the opportunity to voice their opinion."

Workshops in a Nutshell

Running workshops should be a major part of everyday project life. You should plan to run workshops when critical input is required to your project from a cross-section of people. It is the speediest way to capture requirements from cross-functional communities, for example business, user, technical, financial, personnel and management. In fact the very first step of any project should be an initial workshop to define the scope of work.

A workshop is different to a meeting. A workshop should be a high-powered information-gathering session that is formally coordinated by a facilitator. A properly run workshop will meet the following objectives:

❑ All participants have a high degree of input (and are usually exhausted by the end of the session!)
❑ All critical information has been gathered, captured, documented and presented back to all participants
❑ Consensus has been achieved.

When to Run Workshops

If possible, you should try to run workshops when any of the following topics need to be discussed in relation to your project:

- ☑ Defining business or project requirements
- ☑ Corporate visioning, corporate direction, goals, critical business success factors
- ☑ Process changes or process definition – current "As Is" and future "To Be" processes
- ☑ Technical roadmap – environments, standards, strategic applications etc.
- ☑ Organisational changes – process impact, HR implications, training, unions etc.
- ☑ Risk assessment – issue and risk identification, categorisation, mitigation plans etc.

Workshop Outputs

The following lists the documents that should be created and/or updated after the workshop is completed:

Workshop Documents
Workshop notes – fully documented notes on everything that was said at the session.
Updated requirements matrix (see Chapter 6).
Issues and assumptions log.
Action list with names assigned to every action.
Agenda for follow-on workshops.
Scope or design document update (see Chapter 9 and Chapter 10).

Workshop Must Dos

Task	Description
Reserve a room	It is best if the room has lots of wall space to hang flipchart sheets and a projection system.
Make arrangements for food and refreshments	Agree food and delivery times and locations.
Organise flipcharts (preferably two)	Don't forget markers, coloured post-its, tape etc.
Think about an ice-breaker	This works well, especially if the group doesn't know each other.
Arrange "bribes"	Fill a fruit bowl and scatter treats and sweets around the room – this keeps the energy levels up!
Prepare the kick-off	❑ Introductions, e.g. get everyone to declare their name, role and expectations for the session.

	☐ Workshop ground rules, e.g. phones off, only one speaker at a time, full participation, time keeping, ask questions etc. ☐ Workshop objectives, i.e. what you are going to do and how. ☐ Questions.
Assign roles and responsibilities to your team	Everyone on the delivery team (i.e. the team running the workshop) should have one or more roles. There should never be time when your team are just sitting around staring into space! Make sure you have the following roles assigned (one person can play many of these roles): ☐ Facilitator – this person runs the session ensuring the topics on the agenda are covered. The facilitator must be seen to be objective and neutral ☐ Facilitator assistant and general do-gooder (GDG) – this person helps with flipcharts, hands out documentation, markers, tape etc. ☐ Scribes and note takers – practice the concept of timely, zero-loss learning. Always make sure everything is efficiently captured online. Have at least one scribe on a laptop 100% of the time during all sessions. This person is responsible for capturing notes on all important conversations, decisions and issues, as well as duplicating what is on the flipcharts: – Requirements matrix filler – this person should be updating the requirements matrix online during the sessions – Process flow filler – this person should be creating and updating the process flow diagrams during the session ☐ Technical interest – this person will listen for and focus on any technical implications for the project that may arise during the session ☐ Business interest – this person will listen for and focus on any business implications for the project that may arise during the session and ensure that the session stays focused on supporting the overall business vision.

Warning: No matter how limited the resources never run a workshop on your own. Always have at least one other experienced team member in the room with you. Two people can remember much better than one and can capture information much better than one!

We have listed some tips below, which will help you to be a great facilitator:

How to Be a Great Facilitator

Facilitator Tips	Description
Make eye contact	❑ A couple of seconds per person. ❑ Be sure to look at everyone.
Movement	❑ Don't stand still for too long. ❑ Get close to your audience.
Get everyone involved	Ask, "Could I have a response from ... (side of room, table, group)."
Use your voice	❑ Use volume to keep people's attention. ❑ Change tone to keep people's interest.
Keep reading your audience	It's OK to stop the meeting if: ❑ There is an issue that needs to be resolved before going ahead ❑ The audience is tired, lost or unfocused. Consider taking a break if necessary.
Handle difficult behaviour	❑ Make eye contact with the person. ❑ Stand/sit close to the person. ❑ Speak to the person at break. ❑ To get buy-in give them a "role" to play. ❑ Sometimes the group may take care of it for you!
Use different types of tools and methods	<table><tr><th>Tools</th><th>Methods</th></tr><tr><td>Flipcharts Overheads Video Audio Multimedia</td><td>Lecture style Individual exercises Small group discussions Role plays Case studies Simulations</td></tr></table>
Ask open-ended questions	Yes/no answers often don't help; for example, ask, "What questions do you have?" rather than, "Does anyone have any questions?"
Know your audience	Remember to provide the information that your audience requires (not the information that you want to give).
Everyone is important	Make sure that everybody feels included and that their input is valued.
Don't call on specific people	Try not to call on people directly because it can put them on the spot.

Workshops should run no longer than 6 hours in a day	Allow 30–45 minutes for lunch and two 10-minute breaks in the morning and one in the afternoon. Always allow 30 minutes before kick-off to prepare your team. Finish workshops at 3:30 p.m.; this allows your team to format all information captured in the workshop and your attendees can also catch up on their own work or research any further information that might be required.
Capture appropriate comments on flipcharts	This makes the attendees feel they have input which will help gain consensus.
Never disagree with any input	All ideas are welcome in a workshop environment.
Capture issues/concerns and actions on separate flipchart sheets	Have flipchart sheets ready prepared stuck on the wall entitled "Issues/Concerns" and one entitled "Actions". You won't get side tracked as a result. It means if someone does raise an issue you can park it and not spend too much time discussing it during the workshop.
Don't use yellow or red markers to capture requirements on flipcharts	Yellow can't be seen and red is upsetting! Use at least two different marker colours on your flipcharts.
Be very strict on time keeping	Enforce penalties to latecomers, e.g. sing a song!
Be aware not to allow one person to "hog" the session and ensure full participation from everyone	Also watch out for non-participants and make sure they participate.
Do not show emotion or try to force your own ideas	Remember, the facilitator is neutral!
For some topics that require a bit of thought and team work, do not try to facilitate this onto a flipchart	Divide the participants into groups and, within a given time-frame, get them to document their ideas onto post-its, which they then post onto a flipchart. A nominated leader can present their findings back to the group. This is particularly useful when defining future "To Be" process flows or future user requirements.

Tip: Maintain a high energy level – the facilitator sets the tone for the session and must display an active, energetic style. Because it is sometimes difficult for one person to maintain this high energy level all day, you should consider assigning different facilitators for the morning and afternoon sessions. As PM you should ensure that all team members facilitate at some stage. Also if you feel your facilitator is not managing the group well, take a break and switch over – you cannot afford to waste a workshop on poor facilitation.

It Could Happen to you ...

Check that Room!

A very nervous facilitator fell head over heels at the top of a room when, during a difficult and tense technical session, he sat back onto a small table which catapulted him backwards, resulting in a "facilitated" heap at the top of the room! It certainly broke the ice, but when facilitating always check your equipment beforehand.

CHAPTER 5

Process Flow

"Users will only answer the questions you ask and nothing more. It's what you don't ask that hurts you!"

Process Flow Diagrams (PFDs) in a Nutshell

The first step in defining or scoping any project is to model and analyse the business processes onto Process Flow Diagrams (PFDs). The process flows detail the day-to-day activities within an organisation. PFDs tend to provide people with a common language or reference point when dealing with a project or process. They provide an excellent method of documenting processes and are critical when analysing how various business units, departments or functional groups operate together. Strategic improvement often requires some form of change to existing processes. Sometimes processes can even be eliminated! Defining the business process flows is a critical step in determining what is in the scope of a project.

It is best to present your business process flows by graphical representation. As a PM you need to focus on two key elements in process flow identification:

1. The current "As Is" process models
2. The future/innovated "To Be" process models.

Process Flow Representation

In the real world projects are typically run with limited resources, time-frames and budgets. Process flow representation can become a very complicated exercise when topics such as activities, triggers, events, inputs/outputs, key metrics and key sub-activities are thrown in for each process. You also hear about different types of process modelling activities, different types of charts, i.e. top down, work flow etc. Depending upon your project type you must assess the level of detail your process flows represent. For example, projects for manufacturing environments will require extremely detailed and complex process flow representation.

In general, however, process flow representation should be as simple as possible. Don't worry too much about the shapes of your boxes and connectors. It is the content of the actual boxes that counts and the notes you document for each process flow that are critical.

Depending on your preference you can use an automated tool that dynamically generates diagrams or a specific flow chart software package to document your processes yourself.

Warning: The process flows drive out and validate the content of the requirements matrix (see Chapter 6). The business processes that you represent for a project are key as they also represent the boundaries of the scope of the project. This is very important to remember: if a process is not represented in the scope document of a project then that process is deemed "out of scope". As PM you must be extremely vigilant in ensuring you have captured all relevant processes that will affect your project.

Creating your PFDs

- ✓ Create, document and review the current "As Is" process flows. Identify and document the day-to-day scenarios on how a process currently operates.
- ✓ Verify each process flow is correct with an expert user and make changes where necessary.
- ✓ Then create the future "To Be" process flows. To get the best "To Be" process flows assume no restrictions with budget, system, personnel and time; then cut back where necessary.
- ✓ Review "To Be" flows – determine what steps can be added, eliminated and improved through automation or innovation.

✓ Refine and document the "To Be" business flows. For each process flow diagram you should document the following information:
- Diagram of the process – your PFDs
- Brief description of the process
- Changes required for it to happen, for example organisational, technical, personnel
- Identification of the automated and manual steps
- Issues
- Assumptions.

✓ Test the "To Be" processes by walking through a few real-life scenarios representing a "day in the life" of the user.

✓ When all of the process flow diagrams are complete, the processes should be validated against the most common daily user scenarios to ensure that no processes were missed, are deemed redundant or are no longer required.

Tip:
- ❏ Don't spend too much time on the current "As Is" business flows. The bulk of the time spent on business process discussions should be used for the future "To Be" business process flows.
- ❏ Keep your process flow diagrams up to date. They will become very useful during a design phase and will become the basis for the UAT scenarios.

How to Present your Process Flows

This is how we typically model the business processes for IT projects; it works, it's easy to interpret and it captures the critical information. Remember, don't worry too much about the symbols (as they vary per package used); it's the information you capture that matters.

Symbol	Description
⬭	A start terminator represents the beginning of the process at that point.
Activity	The actual activity of work, i.e. the task. Here is how you show a manual activity, i.e. without any automatic/system intervention.

Activity Auto	Here is how you show an automatic/system-aided activity. (Note: some may be a mixture of both, i.e. some manual and auto steps – in this case shade as auto!)
Application/System Name	Make sure to mention which application/system is involved in the task.
Decision Point	There is usually only one output arrow from each box. Otherwise it may require a decision diamond. A decision point is a branch at which the system or user must decide whether the process should continue and/or which path should be followed. Typically a yes/no question.
1 Connector	A connector indicates that the process is not complete but continues on another page or process. **Tip:** identify each process with a number.
Stop	A stop terminator represents the end of the process at that point.

It Could Happen to you ...

Process Flow Pests!

When on a major project for a large insurance firm a very detailed business analyst from the customer team decided that she did not like how the IT delivery team had represented the process flow diagrams. So while working late one evening she decided to rearrange all of them into what she deemed "more cosmetically presentable" flows.

What she failed to notice was that every shaded "box" contained critical information and by rearranging them she managed to lose the key technical details! Needless to say the delivery team were very thankful they had followed back-up procedures! From that point forward a secret password was added to all their documents and clear ownership was assigned.

....

Appendix 5.1: **Sample Process Flow for Customer Relationship Management Solution***

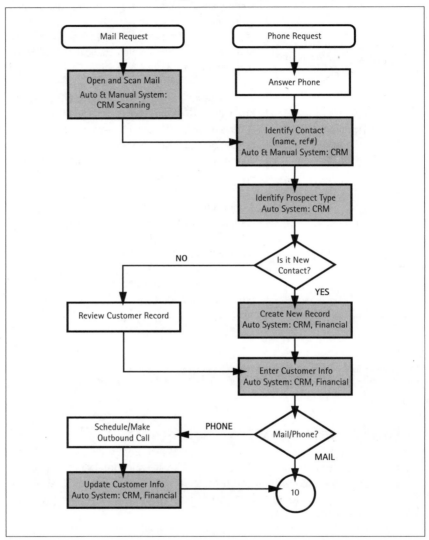

* This is a "Phone Request for Information" to a call centre.

CHAPTER 6

Requirements Matrix

"If you put gobbledygook in your system nothing comes out but gobbledygook. But this gobbledygook, having cost a fortune is now irrefutable and it's a brave person who dares to criticise it!"

Requirements Matrix in a Nutshell

The requirements matrix is a pictorial map of the requirements of a project. It is the snapshot of your complete project and will be invaluable to you and your customer. This is the most critical tool of any project. A requirements matrix should be started at project inception. As requirements are captured, each requirement is entered onto the matrix and then rated high, medium or low based upon business benefit, technical complexity and organisational readiness. Requirements are grouped together by functional area, for example "Reporting" or "Billing".

The matrix is also a very valuable tool for product companies who need a graphical view of the complete set of functionality their product offers.

How do you Create a Requirements Matrix?

As a PM you need to get your team to build a requirements matrix using these steps:

1. Fill in the left-hand column of matrix with all requirements grouped by functional area or business unit. Sample requirements include: human resources, customer service, billing, operations, system administration, reporting etc. (larger functional groups can be broken down further)

2.   Prioritise the requirements. When prioritising each cell put a high, medium or low rating. We typically use the following order:
     – Business benefit first
     – Technical complexity second
     – Organisational readiness third
3.   Phase the requirements.

See Figure 6.1 for an example of requirements defined for a human resources system. Note: Do not analyse the ratings too closely as many different parameters would apply to different organisations in terms of their technical structure, business focus and organisational readiness.

Tip: As a PM you must define up front the rating definitions for business benefit, technical complexity and organisational readiness for your delivery and customer team. Here is an example of business benefit ratings:

High (H) Requirements that are critical to the business that the customer, for example, cannot do their job without.

Medium (M) Requirements that will improve the way business activities are performed, i.e. the requirement is important but there is a possible work around.

Low (L) Requirements that are "nice to have", i.e. there is no real business impact if they are not included.

The exercise of running a requirement through each of these filters, business benefit, technical complexity and organisational readiness, causes very lively discussions but it becomes obvious which requirements are really necessary.

When you phase your requirements use the 80/20 rule as often as possible, i.e. 20 per cent of the pain = 80 per cent of the gain, then the requirement is Phase 1!

Warning: You should be concerned if estimates for Phase 1 of any project indicate that it is going to take longer than 9 months end to end, i.e. scope to rollout. If your project is longer than this it may not be strategic by the time it is rolled out. You should try to phase a project so that all critical requirements and quick wins can be implemented in a maximum of a 6 to 9 month time-frame.

Figure 6.1: Sample Requirements Matrix for Human Resources (HR) System

		1	2	3	4	5	6	7	8	9	10
A	HR	View employee historical details	Auto-generate attendance from attendance sheets	View personal details online	View new staff conditions	Generate security tags and IDs	View terms of employment	Track and monitor all types of leave	Send attendance sheets via e-mail	Display all benefits & concessions	Post job information
		H/L/H	H/M/L	H/L/M	H/L/L	H/M/L	H/L/H	H/H/L	H/L/L	H/M/L	H/L/H
B	HR	Store and update resumes	Auto-generate standard letters	Track training information, plan & schedule	View training records	Track pay scales	Link pay scales with payroll	Track annual reviews online	View organisational information and auto-generate org. charts	Track inter/intra-departmental personnel comparisons	Record and display advertisements
		H/M/H	H/L/M	H/L/L	M/L/M	M/L/H	M/H/M	M/L/H	M/H/H	M/H/L	M/L/H
C	HR	Allow access per user profile	Record exit interview information	Auto-generate establishment lists per dept	Add comments to personnel information	View contractor information and history	Update manpower and succession planning	Create online link recruitment agencies, advertisement agencies etc.	Create reports with trend analysis (see Reports)		
		M/M/M	M/L/H	M/H/H	L/L/H	L/L/L	L/M/L	L/H/L	L/H/H		

Major requirements group (business unit or functional group)

Individual requirement

High business benefit
Medium technical complexity
Low organisational readiness
(lack of discipline of completion of attendance sheets)

Shading indicates phasing phase 1 is black later phases are shown in progressively lighter shades i.e. Phase 2 is grey and phase 3 is white. You choose!

A Warning on Cell Definitions

If your cell definitions are vague in any way, this will impact your estimates and your project. Let's look at an example. Below is a typical requirements row for reporting functionality defined in a scope phase. This reporting row is actually quite dangerous!

Reporting	Customer reports	Recent installations reports	All projects status	Cancelled customer reports	Call statistics reports
	H/M/L	H/M/L	L/L/L	H/L/L	H/L/L

When defining requirements use a verb to ensure accuracy and a clearer definition of the requirement. At a closer look – there is a lot of information missing. Let's look at the very first cell, "Customer reports". A lot of questions need to be answered, including:

❑ How many customer reports, and what type, are actually required?
❑ Do you need to print this report?
❑ Do you need to filter this report?
❑ Do you need to create this report?
❑ Do you need to export this report and if so in what format?
❑ Do you need to edit this report?
❑ Do you need to merge this report?
❑ Are there different views of this report?

Here is how it should look: one cell has now been expanded into seven cells and the business benefit, technical complexity and organisational readiness identified for each requirement. As PM you are now in a much better position to estimate.

Reporting	View new customer report	Print new customer report	Filter new customer report	Create new customer report	Export new customer report to a spreadsheet	Edit new customer report etc.	Merge new customer report
	H/M/L	H/L/H	H/M/L	L/L/L	H/L/L	H/M/L	H/H/H

Another issue is how well each cell is documented. Often teams tend not to document these requirement descriptions well enough. All requirement descriptions should be documented immediately after a session; otherwise you will forget information. Or indeed, if a customer submits a requirement, ask them to document it. Requirements should be documented using the following headings:

- ☑ Summary of requirement
- ☑ Affected business processes
- ☑ User profiles
- ☑ Special features, for example sorting, calculation etc.
- ☑ Rules
- ☑ Business benefit (description and rating H/M/L)
- ☑ Organisational impact (description and rating H/M/L)
- ☑ Data and data source
- ☑ Systems accessed/updated
- ☑ Cost implications, for example new tool etc.
- ☑ Time-frame required
- ☑ Issues and assumptions.

If you document all of the above information for each cell in your matrix, you will be in a very good position to estimate the project and deliver on time and within budget!

It Could Happen to you ...

Details, Details, Details!

A PM made the fatal error of simply putting a cell in the requirements matrix called "Audit reports". The customer assured the PM that there were very few and that they were really quite simple, which the PM believed. Of course when the customer really thought about it, there were more than a few and some were indeed quite complex. The audit report became a nightmare.

The moral of this story is "The devil is in the detail"; use your assumptions list – for example the team should have documented an assumption that "at a maximum there will only be four audit reports and they are of medium technical complexity". At least any further reports could then be appended with cost or time implication added on, thereby taking the pressure off the teams.

CHAPTER 7

Project Justification: Business Case and PoV

"Many projects would not have been started if the truth had been told about the cost and timescale!"

Business Case in a Nutshell

IT projects are typically born out of a desire to improve ways of doing business. This usually means looking at the way people work and implementing process and system improvements. IT projects are not just about producing a product or a solution but ensuring that business benefits to support the organisation's business direction are realised. To ensure this happens, all projects should start with the project overview (PoV) question-naire and that then feeds into the business case. The business case is usually completed during the scope phase.

The business case is an essential piece of project work that supports the executive decision-making process. It is needed to help establish the project ground rules and acts as a basis for all critical project decisions. Most important-ly the business case is a PM's essential tool in managing a project's scope, budget and duration. Typically for IT projects a business case should prove that the new or improved application would do one or more of the following:

❑ Improve productivity
❑ Decrease costs
❑ Increase revenue.

Without a supporting business case, a project will most likely never be approved or successfully implemented. As PM you should try to have a business case expert assigned to your project, especially during its earlier stages.

You should also ensure that you run a PoV meeting with all interested parties before a project is even submitted for approval. A PoV meeting is a critical meeting where all crucial aspects of the project are assessed before any further time or effort is afforded to it.

Project Overview (PoV)

A PoV is a customisable questionnaire that should be completed by a cross-functional team (for example sales, operations, finance, HR and management) before commencement of any project type, whether it is a project for an internal customer or for an external customer. Responsibility for running a PoV can vary; ideally the person responsible for the quality of all projects (for example operations manager, IT manager, QA manager) should ensure it gets completed. Information captured in the PoV questionnaire will serve many valuable purposes.

Goals of the PoV

The following outlines the goals of a PoV:

- ☑ To assess a project in detail and determine its viability
- ☑ To ensure project success
- ☑ To increase "win rate" of customer projects (for external projects)
- ☑ To assess project, business, organisational and technical needs, issues and assumptions
- ☑ To determine if it is worth spending time and resources on the project
- ☑ To more effectively align business development with:
  - Delivery capabilities
  - Target goals
  - Customer needs.

PoV Questionnaire Topics

Your PoV questionnaire should cover the following areas:

Area	Description
Project background	Information is captured concerning how the project is being positioned.
Project planning	What project planning is in place to ensure successful delivery?
External influences	Information here relates to the customer environment, expectations, assumptions etc. and their impact.

Internal influences	What is the team structure used in the planning of the project?
Technology	What is the current and future technical direction of the project?

How Do you Run a PoV?

Running a PoV is not complicated.

> ☑ Simply gather all the right people in a room (or by conference call) for a maximum of one hour. Try to have a representative from the following areas present:
> - Operations, i.e. PM, TL, technical architect
> - Finance, i.e. a person who can assess high-level cost of a project
> - Management, i.e. a person with an overall view of a project's direction and ultimately sign-off
> - Human resources, i.e. a person to assess personnel and potential training requirements.
> ☑ Quickly walk through a PoV questionnaire (customise the sample one below) and answer all the questions.
> ☑ Once this is complete everyone will have a clearer understanding of the project, its potential benefits, team requirements, risks, costs and technologies.
> ☑ A decision can then be made if the team decides to proceed with the project or indeed if it is even worth doing at all!

Warning: A project should pass the due diligence of the PoV process and the business case (scope) phase before it truly becomes a viable and approved project.

A Sample PoV Questionnaire (External and Internal Projects)

You will need to customise this to suit your specific organisational needs. You should begin by documenting who attended. Then for each question below you should document the attendee's responses, any risks or issues and any other pertinent details.

Project Background

Sample Questions to Cover
Company name and contact name/title.
What are the company's annual revenues, employees and how many locations?
In what industry does the company compete?
Briefly describe the initiative.
Does the customer want to re-engineer business processes, organisational design or the culture as part of the project?
Has the customer worked with us on a previous project?
When did the initiative begin and what is the anticipated completion date for the initiative?
What service offering are we proposing?
We are proposing that this phase will last:
The proposed team size is:
How many customer organisations will take part in the project?
To what degree will customer resources be available to us during the project?
Will we be partnering with any other organisations to deliver this offering (i.e. subcontractors, partners, etc.)?
What will be the basis for the proposal pricing?
List all applications considered in scope for the initiative.
List 3 critical success factors that we feel are necessary for the success of this project.
Who is our competition for the project?
How did we learn of this opportunity?
Briefly describe any prior phase for the initiative, noting any external party involvement.
What is the potential for repeat business?
Consequences of system failure (business and technical).
List any critical "drop dead" dates which the customer is facing/planning.
Who are the customer's decision makers for the initiative?
How confident are you that the successful delivery of the proposed services will meet this customer's expectations?
Is this potential in one of our target markets?

Project Planning

Sample Questions to Cover
Has a preliminary project plan been created for this project? (Be sure to attach the project plan.)
Will we be providing the project management for the initiative (as opposed to

| the customer or some other third party)? |
| Has the initial project plan been shared with the customer? |
| Has our methodology and approach been communicated to the customer? |
| List the names and roles of "operations" individuals involved in crafting the proposed solution for this project. |

Internal Influences

Sample Questions to Cover
Given the customer, how confident are you that our resources can deliver the defined deliverables within the proposed time-frame?
List the key roles to be staffed in order to ensure successful delivery of this project.

External Influences

Sample Questions to Cover
What is the customer's budget for the current phase and/or overall initiative?
Indicate the business goal of the initiative.
List all known business plans related to the initiative.
List all known customer expectations regarding the initiative.
How would you describe the scope of change?
Has a business case been built for the initiative?
What area within the business does the customer want addressed?
Has the customer identified specific "best practices" to be achieved as a result of the initiative?
Are the customer's expectations for the initiative realistic?
What is the customer's "anxiety level"?
Are the boundaries, scope and goals of this project clearly identified within the customer organisation?

Technology

Sample Questions to Cover
List the technologies involved.
What package(s) is likely to be used as a component of the final solution?
What application solution is the customer currently running?
What is the customer's current availability demand? (How available must the system be?)
What is the customer's future availability demand? (How available must the system be?)
On what platform is the current solution operating?

| Indicate the selected hardware vendor for the initiative. |
| Indicate the database that will be used for the initiative and an estimate of size. |
| Indicate all applicable technical services included in the proposal. |
| Indicate the technical complexity of the customer's environment. |
| Rate the interface complexity. |
| Indicate the level of data conversion and who is responsible (you, customer or other third party). |
| Indicate who is responsible for data scrubbing responsibilities. |
| Define user groups. |

Creating the Business Case

The business case is a critical piece of work required before a project should commence design and development phases. A high-level business case can be done prior to a scope phase. However, it is really only during a scope phase, when the complete breadth of a project is assessed, that a more detailed business case can be produced. The following are some business case tips:

- ✓ Do not start any project without one – if one does not already exist, build time into the early stages of the project to create one. A project without a business case is a high-risk project.
- ✓ The executive sponsor of a project should own the business case – while it is the responsibility of the PM to ensure one is actually created, it is typically the executive sponsor who has ultimate responsibility for submitting and presenting it to attain approval.
- ✓ Assign "business case" roles within your team:
  - Business case coordinator – usually a business manager who reports to the sponsor. Develops and documents the business case. Will support the executive sponsor and be responsible for getting the document actually delivered and presented.
  - Advisors and contributors – decide who will be impacted by the project and make a representative from each department contribute to the business case, for example IT, finance, HR, marketing, facilities etc.
- ✓ Use the finance department – remember, information necessary for a business case can often be easily accessed in the financial system!

✓ Don't forget the assumptions – typically a business case is created at the start of a project based upon certain assumptions; make sure to document these (issues and assumptions log) and check your assumptions regularly throughout the project.

Sample Business Case Content Checklist

A business case document should cover the following:

✓ The actual business requirement – why the project is needed

✓ Outline design of the solution – what the solution actually is

✓ Alternatives – what are the other options?

✓ Feasibility study – will it work?

✓ Quantitative business benefits – the numbers and figures, what is the pay back?

✓ Qualitative business benefits – the impact upon the organisation, for example improved productivity, efficiency, customer satisfaction, employee loyalty etc.

✓ Cost/benefit analysis

✓ Issues, assumptions and risks

✓ Implementation plan

✓ Actions and next steps.

The following is a sample of the questions that should be addressed in a business case document to ensure a fully supported and viable project. The answers to these questions can be gathered through workshop environments, interviews and questionnaires.

Area	Questions to Answer
The project	❑ Why implement this project? Look at the following reasons: — Survival – can we remain competitive without it? — Legal requirements – are there legal or regulatory requirements that need to be implemented? — Strategic plan – does it support the corporate vision and goals? — Financial – is there are a clear financial gain?

	❑ What happens if we do nothing?
	❑ Other solution options – are there any?
	– What are the strengths and weaknesses of other options?
	– Is there a perfect solution? If so, how close can we get to it?
	– Is there an easier "quick win" solution?
	– How does an alternative solution financially compare?
	– Do we assess 3 or 50 options?
	– Do we go package or in-house?
	❑ What are the administration requirements for the project?
	❑ Do we need new office space, new people, new hardware etc.?
	❑ Are the current accounting systems capable of supporting the new project and its benefits measurement?
	❑ Will new systems be required? If so, can they be done in house? What are the costs?
Management	❑ Who is the driving force behind this project?
	❑ Is there a genuine support for the project?
	❑ What breadth across the organisation actually supports the project?
	❑ Is there a financial management plan for the project that feeds into the benefits analysis?
	❑ Who will manage all the costs – finance office, project team, executive sponsor?
	❑ Have we the appropriate skills to support the project?
	❑ Can the project be phased to deliver early benefit or deferred costs? 80/20 rule?
	❑ Are there constraints?
	❑ Are there special considerations that must be considered (for example, savings in people must show increased benefit and redeployment)?
	❑ What are the risks?
	– Is there a risk-management process/analysis?
	– Is there a cost measurement against each potential risk?
	– How do the risks affect the benefits?
	❑ What management decisions are required?
	❑ What targets are fixed? Do these cover budgets,

	❏	headcount, revenue targets and commission plans?
	❏	How will performance against business be reviewed?
Cost/benefit	❏	Has a payback period been determined?
	❏	Will it exceed the life of the project and if so who will continue to measure it?
	❏	What criteria are being used to judge the benefits or the success of the project?
	❏	What are the benefits?
		— Have they been adequately defined?
		— How do they compare with other solutions?
		— How will the benefits be measured – qualitative and quantitative?
		— Direct cost savings
		— Labour savings
		— Productivity increases
		— Can they be measured?
	❏	Who actually measures them?
	❏	What are the actual costs – project costs and ongoing support costs?
		— Supplier costs
		— Hardware costs
		— Software costs
		— Consultants costs
		— HR costs (hiring etc.)
		— Note: some will need to be estimated, as they are unknowns.
	❏	What is the impact on profit & loss (P&L)?
	❏	What is the impact on cash flow over time?
	❏	What is the impact on the balance sheet (assets and liabilities)?

Tip:

As a PM it is up to you to raise the above questions if you are handed a project without a supporting business case. If there is no business case it is up to you to assign time for one to be done. Remember, good PMs know when to manage projects and when not to!

It Could Happen to you ...

The Quiet Business Analyst

During the late 1990s a lot of our projects were for Dot Coms. Investment was high – everyone was looking for the golden nugget! One particular Dot Com project was for a US retail organisation that planned to set up a Dot Com in Europe. It was our job to scope and design the project and present a technical and strategic roadmap for its implementation. It was a very exciting project for our customer and for us; if successful it would have been big!

During the early days of scoping, the business analyst quietly but consistently questioned the business model. In a very polite non-invasive way he kept pointing out potential issues with the business model and business case. He became very unpopular with our customer and, let's face it, was probably "hushed" by the PM. Big money was spent but the project did not take off. It failed. The reason we learnt months later: the business case and business model did not stack up!

If any member of a delivery team has serious reservations about a project they should be listened to: it's easy to get carried away with what seems like an exciting project!

CHAPTER 8

Project Methodology

"Don't abandon your process in a crisis – successful companies don't!"

Project Methodology in a Nutshell

Project methodology defines the processes and procedures you use to run your project. Having a project methodology means that you have an agreed standard on how you are going to implement your project. This usually means having a project guideline, project lifecycle, set of project tools, set of project techniques and project templates that are standard across the entire organisation. The key to success is that they are reusable from project to project and are proven to work!

Our research on project management methodologies shows that there are over 50 well-known methodologies, any of which could be applied to software development projects. Some of these methodologies can be divided into:

- ❑ Project management methodologies
- ❑ Software development methodologies
- ❑ System analysis methodologies
- ❑ Others.

This book will not go into any of these! We believe that fundamentally they are all quite similar: the golden rules still apply, i.e. involve the customer, develop in relatively short, iterative cycles, keep it simple, document at the right level and train your team.

As a PM you need to define your project methodology as clearly, concisely and simply as possible. So define a lifecycle that suits your projects and define exactly what documents and template deliverables are required for each phase of your lifecycle.

Don't worry about the hype of all the different methodologies out there; don't panic about having to choose one; most organisations have a mish-mash of different methodologies that they have tweaked to work for them!

What we are giving you in this chapter is a straightforward methodology that has been proven to work worldwide across various customer sectors and across various project types, from the very large to the very small! Use it as your methodology baseline and stick to the key deliverables and rules for each of its phases and your project will succeed.

A Proven Methodology

There are typically two types of software development projects you will manage:

1. Package implementation, which normally demands some element of customisation
2. Purely customised implementation, using tools and programming languages to develop your solution.

There is a lifecycle for each and these are detailed below. Every member of your organisation should know the lifecycle and and deliverables for each lifecycle phase.

The first step for a PM is defining/understanding the lifecycle that fits into your organisation. The golden rule is that the lifecycle applies to all projects within the organisation no matter how big or small.

It should be noted, however, that projects can be initiated at different stages of the lifecycle. This should only happen if you are satisfied that the deliverables and graduation criteria for the previous phase have been delivered. Also project phases vary in length from project to project, depending upon the size of the project and the quality and amount of information you have at the start of the project lifecycle.

Customised Project Implementation vs Package Implementation

Some applications are coded from scratch, using a set of development tools and coding languages. Other applications are better suited to using an existing package that already provides a solution and it is the team's job then to tailor the package to suit the customer's needs. Customer Relationship Management (CRM) applications are typically based upon package solutions. It probably doesn't make sense to build an application from scratch if 70 per cent of it exists already in a package!

The choice of whether to build or buy is often a hard one and it can take time. To identify a suitable package you need to follow some steps:

- ✓ Research the area
- ✓ Identify the types of package that might be suitable
- ✓ Build a scorecard for yourself, identifying all of your needs
- ✓ Do a preliminary match of packages to your needs and shortlist some packages (talk to vendors)
- ✓ Ask short-listed vendors to create a tailored prototype for you and present to you, your team and the business. Make sure they prototype your typical processes – not theirs!
- ✓ Score all vendors
- ✓ Select the most appropriate one (if any!).

If there are no suitable packages then you are back to building a solution!

The two lifecycles are very similar. For a package solution, instead of designing a solution, you are doing a gap analysis of what is in and out of the package and designing only what is not provided by the package and what needs to be tailored. You may have to change some of your business processes to suit the package too and this should be implemented throughout the business.

During development you are building the customised elements of the project and configuring the package to suit your needs. The difference between Figure 8.1 and Figure 8.2 is self-explanatory.

Figure 8.1: **Customised Project Lifecycle**

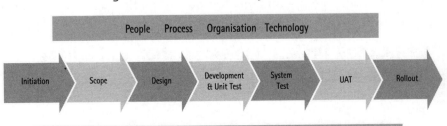

Figure 8.2: **Package Implementation Project Lifecycle**

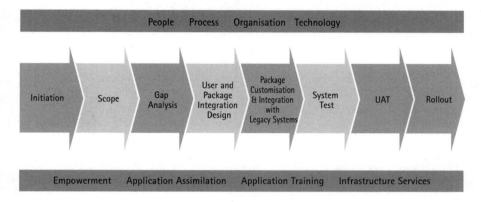

The following is a brief description of the major stages.

Project Initiation

This is the phase where your organisation identifies a new project and then decides whether it is appropriate to go forward with it:

- ❑ Is there a need for the project?
- ❑ Does it make sense for the business?
- ❑ Is there a business case for it and does it stack up?
- ❑ Can you live without it?
- ❑ Will you be able to resource it?
- ❑ Are there the skills and technologies available to implement it?

All of these questions and more need to be considered.

To make such a decision we recommend that you use the following process:

- ✓ Get the appropriate people in the room who can make a decision (sales, finance, operations, techies, human resources etc.)
- ✓ Step through the PoV questionnaire to see how appropriate the project is for you (see Chapter 7)
- ✓ Agree to begin the project or not!

Sometimes there may be a proposal process associated with the project, for example if you work for a consulting firm. You may need to build a proposal, submit it and then implement the project if you are successful. Here is a recommended proposal process:

Figure 8.3: **Recommended Proposal Process**

RFP/RFI received/sales call					You've won the business! Start Project
Initiate	Hold PoV	Staff the Team	Build Proposal	Submit Proposal	Hold Project Norming
❑ Proposal review ❑ Preparation – research etc.	❑ Review with PoV team, Ops, HR etc. ❑ Agree whether to submit proposal ❑ Agree approach (use PoV checklist to run meeting)	❑ Assign team	❑ Norm team ❑ Assign roles and responsibilities ❑ Research ❑ Write proposal ❑ Review with appropriate team	❑ Attend meetings etc. as required ❑ Provide additional information as required	❑ Assign PM ❑ Staff the team ❑ Create project plan ❑ Begin the scoping phase ❑ Work with the customer ❑ Work with external suppliers ❑ Etc.

Scope

The scope phase is the definition of a project. It identifies the breadth of the requirements to be completed to deliver a project within a defined time-frame. It should be the first phase of every project. We recommend that you do not start a design phase without having scoped – even if it is just for a day.

During this phase, you get to ask all of the important questions:

- ✓ You analyse your customer's business environment to identify process and organisational changes that must be made to deliver the project
- ✓ You identify the targeted users, what their needs are and what essential functions the application must perform
- ✓ You define the technical architecture at a high level, look at the technology choices and possibly begin a process of investigation/selection of tools and packages
- ✓ You evaluate the customer's network and security infrastructure

☑ Most importantly, you build your requirements matrix (see Chapter 6) that details all of the functionality to be implemented.

Deliverables
❏ Scope document.
❏ Scope presentation.

Design

Whereas scope defines the breadth of a project, design defines the depth and ultimately the overall solution for the project, from both a business and a technical perspective. Each piece of functionality identified in the scope is investigated and drilled into and the business and/or technical solution is designed and documented in detail. This means the user interface and technical architecture to support the overall solution are created and documented, and accurate time-frames and costs can be provided to your customer.

Design focuses on the following specific areas:

☑ User design (business requirements and user interfaces)
☑ Technical design (technical solution, performance requirements, security, system administration etc.)
☑ Estimation and project planning.

Deliverables
❏ Design document.
❏ Design presentation.

Development

The development phase of your project is the phase where your application is finally created. During this phase you should have very few surprises – the scope of the project should be totally clear and the "how to" should be detailed in the design document and just require implementation. Each developer gets to build, unit test and integrate their code into the overall application.

Deliverables

❑   A working application.
❑   Supporting documentation:
  –   Development document – this is the design document updated to reflect any changes that occurred during development
  –   Issues, risks and assumptions list
  –   Testing and rollout plan
  –   User's guide (if required)
  –   Programmer's guide (if required)
  –   System management guide.
❑   Customer training – the customer needs to become familiar with the application and learn how to use it, to prepare them for the User Acceptance Testing (UAT) phase of the project and ultimately rollout.

System Test

When all the modules of the project have been created and unit and integration tested, i.e. development is completed, an overall system test must take place. This tests the entire application end-to-end, from the start through to the end of each process. It tests all the technologies and tools that have been employed and all of the code developed. A set of scenarios must be created that will test both user scenarios and technology scenarios. During system test you should employ both positive and negative testing, i.e. testing the way it should work as well as testing the way it should not work. Performance testing will also take place at this point to ensure the application is reaching the response levels expected by the customer.

Deliverables

❑   A system-tested application.
❑   Supporting documentation.

User Acceptance Testing (UAT)

UAT is the phase of a project that all development teams dread and live for at the same time. It is when the users get to test the application against what they originally designed. (Note: your design document is key during this phase to confirm what the users asked for!) UAT is the hardest and trickiest phase and it can be the most explosive! The users go through the application with a fine-tooth comb, trying both positive and negative testing and testing against pre-defined data and checking expected results. At the end of this phase the users should sign off the application.

Deliverables
❑   A signed-off application.
❑   List of agreed outstanding bugs (should only have low and cosmetic bugs outstanding).

Rollout

This is the "go live" phase. You can either do a pilot rollout – where the application is rolled out within one small group for a while and is then incrementally rolled out across the organisation; or a full-blown rollout – where the application is rolled out across the organisation in one go. Depending on your choice, your rollout time-frame and plan will be affected. The rollout phase typically happens over a weekend.

Deliverables
❑   Live application.
❑   Supporting documentation.

IT COULD HAPPEN TO YOU ...

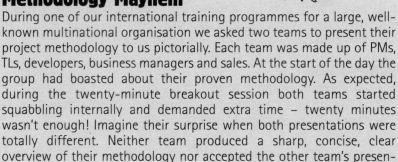

Methodology Mayhem

During one of our international training programmes for a large, well-known multinational organisation we asked two teams to present their project methodology to us pictorially. Each team was made up of PMs, TLs, developers, business managers and sales. At the start of the day the group had boasted about their proven methodology. As expected, during the twenty-minute breakout session both teams started squabbling internally and demanded extra time – twenty minutes wasn't enough! Imagine their surprise when both presentations were totally different. Neither team produced a sharp, concise, clear overview of their methodology nor accepted the other team's presentation!

Two teams from one organisation should, in ten minutes, be able to present a clear picture of their project lifecycle listing the deliverables for each phase. Two teams from the one organisation should present the exact same picture!

CHAPTER 9

Scope

"At the core of every large project are small projects screaming to be delivered – it's these projects that are the golden nuggets."

Scope in a Nutshell

The scope phase is the definition of a project. It identifies the breadth of the requirements to be completed to deliver a project within a defined time-frame. It should be the first phase of every project. It is important not to start designing without having scoped – even if it's just for a day!

Scoping is often the most underestimated exercise and depending on the project in question it can take from a day to a couple of months. The best scoping results are achieved through workshop environments with cross-functional teams representing all potential stakeholders of the project.

Scope Deliverables

There are typically two deliverables from a scope phase:

1. Scope document
2. Scope presentation – you should aim to have a formal feedback presentation upon completion of a scope; ideally anyone involved in the scope should attend.

Scope Document

Below is our recommended scope document table of contents that ensures you cover all aspects of the scope phase.

Introduction	
	Executive overview (project time-frames and costs*)
	The scope process
	Project vision, objectives and deliverables
	Project participants
Business Context	
	Introduction
	Business drivers
	Business corporate goals
	Critical success factors
	Business vision
	Project goals
	Key performance measures
Process Flows	
	Introduction
	High-level business process flows
Requirements	
	Introduction
	Requirements matrix
	Requirements descriptions
	- Requirement description
	- Prioritisation rating
	- Phase (to be implemented in)
	- Notes
	- Issues
	- Assumptions
Technical Architecture	
	Introduction
	About the architecture
	Application architecture
	Current data sources
	New data requirements
	Current environments
Business Case	
	Introduction
	Quantitative business benefits
	Qualitative business benefits
	Estimated project costs
	Cost/benefit analysis
Next Steps	
	Introduction
	Recommendations (delivery options)
	High-level project plan

	Detailed project costs (estimated hardware, software, HR etc.)
	Roles and responsibilities during design
Issues, Assumptions and Risks	
	Issues
	Assumptions
	Risks
Appendices	
Glossary	

* Project costs should include actual next phase costs (for example design) and estimated costs for the complete project. The estimated costs should demonstrate high-end vs low-end options, for example build or buy an IT solution.

Presentation

It is important that this presentation is presented at the appropriate level to your sponsor, business team etc. Remember: executives want the bird's eye view.

Your presentation should cover the following topics:

- ❑ Introduction – overview of the scope, the process used, who was involved, when it took place
- ❑ Business context – the business landscape surrounding the project
- ❑ Process flows – a summary of the recommended "To Be" flows
- ❑ User requirements – the requirements needed to deliver the project
- ❑ Technical architecture – high-level technical landscape
- ❑ Delivery options – time-frames, teams and technologies
- ❑ Business case – cost options and justification
- ❑ Next steps – steps to move forward
- ❑ Any identified issues, assumptions and risks.

Scope Must Dos

1. Define scope objectives ✓
2. Define scope duration ✓
3. Define your team and time commitments ✓
4. Prepare your team ✓
5. Create your scope plan ✓
6. Run your scope ✓

7. Estimate your project ✓
8. Document your findings ✓
9. Present your findings ✓

1. Define Scope Objectives

The main objectives of a scope phase are to:

❑ Define the breadth of the requirements (*not* the depth!)
❑ Determine the business justification of the project
❑ Get buy-in from management, users, business and technical personnel
❑ Determine any technical implications and potential solutions
❑ Get a high-level estimate for the budget and the duration of the entire project end to end
❑ Get a fixed budget and duration for the next phase, for example design
❑ Assess the risk of the project.

2. Define Scope Duration

Determine firstly what is in the scope phase by identifying whom and what processes in the organisation will be affected by it. The number of processes and business units that are impacted will help you determine how long the official scope phase will last.

Depending on the process complexity you will typically need to allocate the following time per process in your scope schedule:

❑ High process complexity: 2–3 days
❑ Medium process complexity: 1 day
❑ Low process complexity: 1/2 day
❑ Simple process complexity: 2 hours.

Remember to add appropriate time for technical discussions, technical assessment of requirements matrix, documentation, estimation and presentation of findings.

Do these estimates seem low? Bear in mind these estimates assume the following:

- ❏ The right subject-matter experts are in the room for each process
- ❏ There is a strict schedule on what you want to discuss for each process
- ❏ Every process is broken down to its simplest level.

3. Define your Team and Time Commitments

To ensure your scope phase is a success you need to involve the right people – the right people from the customer side and the right people that will deliver the project, i.e. the delivery team.

Customer Team (mostly part-time)

- ❏ Visionary – the person who knows what the end result should be.
- ❏ Executive sponsor – the person who is rubber-stamping the whole project (this can also be the visionary). This is a key role, as unless your project has an executive sponsor you will not receive the support and priority you need to get the job done.
- ❏ Business PM – someone who will manage the customer team and coordinate with the delivery team.
- ❏ Business experts – there must be a knowledgeable representative from each of the business areas that will be impacted by the project.
- ❏ Users – get your end users involved (fight for the most knowledgeable ones!).
- ❏ Technologists – the technology experts who may have to develop and implement the solution.

Delivery Team

- ❏ PM – responsible for the delivery of a project (full-time).
- ❏ Business analyst – responsible for the business impact, i.e. process flows and business case (full-time).
- ❏ TL – responsible for the technical solution (full-time).
- ❏ Technical architect – the technical visionary for the entire organisation (part-time).
- ❏ Developers – responsible for requirements gathering and documenting (full-time).
- ❏ Database administrator – responsible for defining the data architecture (part-time).

- ❏ Sales/account manager – responsible for executive customer management, used for escalation of issues (part-time).
- ❏ Finance – helps with the business case (part-time).

4. Prepare your Team

We often find that it is hard to "sell" preparation time into a project. The reason is that people do not understand what actually should be done during this time. Bad preparation means a bad project. Try to allocate anything from two to five days.

Preparation Activities

- ❏ Hold kick-off meeting
- ❏ Prepare customer:
  - – Agree workshop agendas and time commitments
  - – Send out questionnaires and assign deadline return dates
  - – Gather all process documentation and create first cut of "As Is" and/or "To Be" process flow diagrams and requirements matrix.
- ❏ Prepare impact assessment documentation:
  - – Technical questionnaires: environment assessment (see sample technical questionnaire in Appendix 9.1)
  - – Organisational assessment: resources, training, culture etc.
- ❏ Assess other ongoing projects that might be impacted and liaise with other PMs.
- ❏ Prepare your schedule.
- ❏ Start your issues and assumptions log. (**Remember:** This log stays with you until the project officially ends!)
- ❏ Plan for your scope sessions: workshops, interviews and meetings.

Preparation Kick-Off Meeting

- ❏ Norm your team (see Chapter 3).
- ❏ Define roles and responsibilities for each team member.
- ❏ Present project overview: plan, deliverables, time-frames.
- ❏ Discuss customer background.
- ❏ Discuss:
  - – Past projects that were similar in nature whether external or internal
  - – Research best-in-class solutions and match them to your project
  - – Lessons learned.

- ❑ Define scope methodology.
- ❑ Demonstrate scope tools, for example requirements matrix, process diagrams etc.
- ❑ Agree scope standards: documentation, version control, naming conventions, security etc.
- ❑ Agree scope deliverables, i.e. presentation and document.
- ❑ Discuss concerns or worries with your team.
- ❑ Define any project administration:
  - Back-up, confidentiality agreements, meetings, hours of work, holidays, finance (expenses, taxis, per diems, training).

5. Create your Scope Plan

Below is a sample one-week scope plan, assuming you will be running a series of workshops. Remember, a scope can be half a day but the important thing is that you must cover all the topics listed in the plan below for every process/business unit affected.

You may gather your information via other means, for example one-on-one interviews and/or questionnaires. It is important, however, to gather all your team together (customer and delivery) to attend an initial scope kick-off meeting, to ensure team consensus.

Monday	Tuesday	Wednesday	Thursday	Friday
9:30am Scope kick-off Introductions and expectations Overview of customer Presentation of scope process Group: Vision, goals, CSFs and business benefits	9:30am Define process improvement / changes Review business process maps Discuss: ❑ Requirements ❑ Constraints ❑ Data sources ❑ Business benefits	9:30am Continue to discuss ❑ Requirements ❑ Constraints ❑ Data sources ❑ Business benefits	9:30am Review requirements matrix Prioritise requirements Prioritise business benefits Analyse and resolve issues	9:30am **FEEDBACK PRESENTATION**
Lunch: 12:30 – 1:00	Lunch: 12:30 – 1:00	Lunch: 12:30 – 1:00	Lunch: 12:30 – 1:00	
1:00 pm Overview of general process Review current business processes	1:00 pm Continue to discuss ❑ Requirements ❑ Constraints ❑ Data sources ❑ Business benefits	1:00 pm Discuss technical complexity Explore architecture, tools, issues, technical standards for current and future environment Discuss database (high-level) Discuss network infrastructure	1:00 pm Documentation	
3:30pm checkpoint	3:30pm checkpoint	3:30pm checkpoint	3:30pm checkpoint	

6. Run your Scope

Where possible we recommend you define the project requirements through workshops. However, often this is not possible and information gathering may happen through one-on-one interviews or questionnaires. Make sure all the topics listed below get addressed.

Scope Kick-Off

This sets the scene for the entire scope process. The full team should attend this session.

Tip: The sponsor should be asked to kick off this session with a few words and deliver the "vision and blessing" for the project. This ensures buy-in from all attendees.

Start the day with a quick kick-off presentation covering:

- ❑ Introductions
- ❑ Agenda
- ❑ Expectation setting – get everyone to give you their expectation on the first day, put it up on the wall and on the last day tick each one off to confirm to them that you have met their expectations
- ❑ Scope overview and process
- ❑ Scope schedule
- ❑ Next steps.

Identify the Business Context, Vision, Goals and Critical Success Factors (CSFs)

This session needs to be tightly controlled as you could talk about it for days! A good PM will come to the session prepared and let the user validate the definitions. With the right people in the room this should not be longer than five hours, and that is for a large project!

- ❑ Business context – determine the company's place within the industry and within the market; who are the players and what are the opportunities?
- ❑ Vision – there may be many vision statements created during the scope, including a vision for the company, a vision for the application, etc.

❑ Goals – help define the vision; what are the goals of the project, for example increase revenue by 40 per cent.
❑ Critical Success Factors (CSFs) – what has to happen in order for the project to be successful?

Identify Current Major Areas of Pain

Have each participant articulate their areas of pain, as it is here you will easily get the start of the user requirement definition and participants love this topic. It will be the most interactive session and the most informative.

Define Process Flows *(see Chapter 5)*

❑ Validate the current "As Is" processes and update them.
❑ Create the future "To Be" processes. Test the "To Be" process-es by walking through a few real-life scenarios representing a "day in the life" of the customer. Remember, if a process is not discussed it is deemed out of scope!

Identify User Requirements and Create your Requirements Matrix *(see Chapter 6)*

You should have created a first cut at an initial requirements matrix during preparation time.

Create your Business Case *(see Chapter 7)*

Hold your Technical Sessions

Here is a sample of the kind of technical information that needs to be gathered and documented during the technical sessions. Just remember that you are in the scope phase not design so it is important to discuss each topic at a broad level.

Technical Session Topics

✓ Conceptual architecture (location of components, two tier, three tier etc.).
✓ Database (sources, currency, quality/accuracy, accessibili-ty, current volumes, anticipated volumes).
✓ Hardware architecture.
✓ Software architecture.
✓ Network.
✓ External systems and connectivity.
✓ Reporting.
✓ Internationalisation.

- ✓ Performance.
- ✓ Security and system administration (back-up, recovery etc.).
- ✓ Impact on current environment, for example operational procedures etc.
- ✓ Short-term/long-term IT initiatives that will impact this application and/or data.
- ✓ User community (total number of end-users, maximum number of concurrent users, growth potential).
- ✓ Review requirements matrix – review requirements matrix and assess the technical complexity of each requirement by marking them high, medium or low. Make sure to document associated issues, assumptions and risks with each requirement.

Prioritise and Phase your Matrix

Run a joint session with all business and technical customers and prioritise and phase requirements. This is the fun session: it is going to be argumentative, demands a lot of facilitation and negotiation but should end with team consensus and agreement on the phasing.

Gathering Requirements by Questionnaires

If gathering user requirements by workshop environment is not feasible, you should get users to document their requirements using the following headings (Note: each individual requirement must be documented):

Requirements Definition

- ✓ Summary of requirement – brief overview of the requirement.
- ✓ Affected business processes – list the business processes that will be affected by the requirement.
- ✓ User profiles – list the users who will be affected or who will need system access to it.
- ✓ Special features – list any special features of the requirements, for example sorting, a calculation etc.
- ✓ Rules – list who, when, how or why the requirement may be used or called upon.
- ✓ Business benefit – identify if the requirement supports the business direction or vision, mark each requirement with a H/M/L rating.
- ✓ Organisational impact – identify what impact the require-

ment may have from an organisational viewpoint, for example will extra PCs be required, will extra training be required, is the organisation ready for the requirement? Assign an organisational readiness rating of H/M/L.

☑ Data and data source – what information is needed for the requirement and where can this information be accessed?

☑ Systems accessed/updated – list the systems that will be impacted by adding or changing the requirement.

☑ Cost implications – list any cost implications by adding the requirement, for example new software, new hardware etc.

☑ Time-frame required – identify a drop-dead date for requirement implementation.

☑ Issues and assumptions – list any known potential problems or assumptions that the requirement is based upon.

7. Estimate your Project *(see Chapter 13)*

Estimate the effort to implement Phase 1 using your requirements matrix. At this point you can give actual cost and time for next phase and low-end to high-end estimates for the complete project.

8. Document your Findings

Create your final document and organise external reviews.

9. Present your Findings

❑ Organise a date for the scope presentation – make sure all relevant parties can attend, especially the sponsor.

❑ Hand out copies of the scope document for review.

❑ Agree a date for document feedback.

❑ Agree next steps and assign actions.

Tip: To ensure sponsor buy-in, try to get the customer team to present sections of the final presentation. It means the customer team is in agreement about the whole direction of the project and your customer is now selling the project and its benefits upwards.

It Could Happen to you ...

The Valley of Despair

The valley of despair is a symptom that typically strikes mid-way through a scope. Scopes start on such a buzz – there is a feeling of excitement and everyone is full of great ideas. You build your ideal matrix. All ideas are great and are captured but then reality strikes in the form of the prioritisation session. Requirements are phased and "Phase 2" becomes a very bad word. People get despondent and enter the valley of despair! They begin to feel that they are not getting everything they asked for (by the way, they shouldn't be either!).

As a PM it is your job to recognise this and motivate and enthuse them again. Let them know this always happens and encourage them to trust you. Tell them they are in "the valley of despair" and that they will get out of it soon!

But how do you get back on track? Make sure you organise your scope feedback presentation, as it is here that everyone gets to see the value of the work done. If this presentation is done properly you will create a buzz about your project again and "bye-bye" valley of despair!

Appendix 9.1: Sample Technical Questionnaire

Areas	Questions
Strategy	❏ Is technology architecture standardised at a corporate level? ❏ Are any major upgrades planned in the foreseeable future? ❏ Does an internet strategy exist?
Infrastructure	❏ What is the current LAN/WAN architecture (diagram) and the component inventory? ❏ Are there currently preferred vendor/partnerships in place involving any of the above or other suppliers? ❏ Is there an infrastructure security policy? (If so can a copy be supplied?) ❏ What is the support structure for the infrastructure? What way is support segmented? ❏ What technologies or vendors are currently used/planned for the following systems? – Routers/switches/hubs – Firewall – hardware – Firewall – software – Cabling – Networking protocols (e.g. TCP/IP) – User accounts/user directory services – Mainframe devices – Unix hardware – Unix software – Server hardware – Desktop operating system – Desktop hardware – ISP/hosting – EDI links.
Desktop	❏ What is the typical operating system for desktops? ❏ What is the typical operating system for laptops? ❏ What are the office automation products used? Do these form part of a suite? ❏ Are there any other standard products installed on a desktop/laptop? ❏ What is the typical type of machine used? ❏ Is software held locally or centrally distributed?

Network Servers	❑ What is the network operating system used?
	❑ What is the typical type of machine used?
	❑ Are any UNIX machines used?
Groupware	❑ Is any Groupware server used?
	❑ What is the version number of the Groupware?
	❑ What modules/types of applications are used?
	❑ What database supports the Groupware?
	❑ What is the e-mail standard?
	❑ Are intranets used?
Application Servers	❑ What is the typical operating system for application servers?
	❑ What is the typical type of machine used?
Database Servers	❑ What is the typical operating system for database servers?
	❑ What is the typical database installed?
	❑ Are any specialist database machines employed?
Mainframes	❑ Who is the typical supplier?
	❑ What is the typical operating system for mainframe computers?
Security	❑ What is the typical security architecture in place?
Telephony	❑ What switch is used?
	❑ Is this switch CTI-able?
	❑ How extensible is this switch?
	❑ What type of video-conferencing equipment and software is used?
Development Architecture	
Strategy	❑ Does your company engage in development of major systems using an internal IT department?
	❑ What is the current architecture of choice (two/three tier customer/server, host based, mainframe etc.)?
	❑ Are there significant legacy systems that used a different architecture?
Host-based Architecture	❑ Who is the supplier of choice?
Customer/ Server Architecture	❑ Is the typical architecture two tier or three tier?
	❑ Are any GUI tools used?
	❑ What is the typical database used?
	❑ What middleware is employed?
	❑ Are any industry standard information exchange protocols used?
Enterprise	❑ What are the vendor packages or technologies supporting

Applications	the following tasks and what standard platforms do they reside upon? - Web servers - Application servers - Databases - Directory services - E-mail - Personalisation services - Indexing and searching - Middleware and business ware - Legacy systems and architecture - Business applications, e.g. financial, CRM etc. - File, content or document management - Groupware/workflow
	In the case of all these major applications using the above technologies, please supply the information specified below: a. What is the architecture of the application (e.g. customer/server vs host based)? b. What operating system does the application run under (in the case of customer/server list both customer and server)? c. What database/flat file architecture does the application use? d. Is the application based on a package or is it custom developed? e. Does the application have a graphical user interface? f. Are there any special hardware/software requirements for users of the application? g. What type of data are stored within this application? h. What are the availability requirements of this application? i. What are the main current issues associated with this application? j. What is the number of concurrent and forecasted users of this application? ❏ What is the support structure for enterprise applications? ❏ What standards are currently planned or in place for web initiative development tools, browsers, specifications, architectures and strategies? ❏ Are there preferred vendor/partnership relationships in place?

❑ What are the current licensing arrangements for existing technologies (components, numbers of users/developers, support etc.)?

❑ Are there external technical considerations for web initiative developments?

❑ What are the current development skill sets within the company?

CHAPTER 10

Design

"Abraham Lincoln reportedly said that, given eight hours to chop down a tree, he'd spend six sharpening his axe!"

Design in a Nutshell

Whereas scope defines the breadth of a project, design defines the depth and ultimately the overall solution for the project, from both a business and a technical perspective. Each piece of functionality identified in the scope is analysed and the business and technical solution is designed and documented in detail. In other words, the user interface (the screens) and the supporting technical architecture are defined and documented. After the design phase accurate time-frames and costs can be provided to your customer. The ultimate deliverable of design is a design document, which is a blueprint for development. This document should be so detailed that any development team can go and develop a solution from it without having attended the design!

Design focuses on the following specific areas:

❑ User design – business requirements, process changes, user interfaces
❑ Technical design – technical solution, performance requirements, security, system administration etc.
❑ Estimation and project planning – development through to rollout time-frames, roles and responsibilities, costs and project specifications.

If the design phase is for a product implementation (as opposed to a completely customised solution) then you must do a gap analysis first. This is where you assess the functionality of the product against your customer's requirements, identify the gaps and then design for those gaps in the product.

The requirements matrix plays a critical role in the design phase. Used correctly, every single requirement will be analysed in detail and estimated correctly for development.

Design Deliverables

There are typically two deliverables from a design:

- ❏ Design document
- ❏ Design presentation – anyone involved in the design should attend this presentation. It is an opportunity to get management and the project sponsor back together to inform them about the project status, for example:
  - If there have been any changes to the functionality originally agreed in the scope
  - Any current issues
  - Definitive cost and time-frames for the remainder of the project.

Design Document

Below is a recommended design document table of contents that ensures you cover all aspects of the design phase.

Executive Overview
Introduction
Project background
Objectives, critical success factors and vision statement
Solution overview
Technical recommendations and high-level architecture
Business benefits
Project costs* and timelines
Acknowledgements (contributors)
Requirements Matrix
Introduction
Requirements matrix
Requirements description
Business Process
Introductions
Business process flows
Business process flow descriptions
User Interface
Introduction
Screen flow
Screen specifications

Object Specifications (if object-oriented solution)
Introduction
Use case specifications
Class specifications
Operation specifications

Function Specifications
Introduction
Function specifications

Algorithms
Introduction
Algorithm specifications

Connectivity
Introduction
External interface specifications
Systems accessed specifications

Reports
Introduction
Report specifications

Data
Overview
Database design (Entity Relationship Diagram)
Database schema
Table specifications
Data dictionary
Database procedures
Data volumes
Class to data mapping

System Architecture
Introduction
Software architecture
Presentation layer
Functionality layer
Data layer
Software architecture diagram
Hardware architecture
Software to hardware mapping
Communication mechanism
Hardware architecture diagram
Network architecture
Network management
Network architecture diagram
Architecture requirements

Development environment
Preliminary production/rollout environment
Major concerns and issues
Performance expectations and requirements
Tool evaluations

System Administration

Database back-ups
System back-ups
Restart and recovery
Logging/error handling
Application administration
Audit trail
System administration
Configuration management
Scheduling
Data back-up and archiving
Disaster recovery
Security

Issues, Assumptions and Risks

Issues
Assumptions
Risks

Plan

Development plan
Pre-production plan
Preliminary test plans
Responsibilities – both the customer and delivery team

Appendices

Glossary (if necessary)
Tools analysis (if applicable)

---

* Project costs should include costs for the complete project. You may, however, demonstrate
high-end vs low-end options.

Tip: Use your design document specifications, especially the user interface chapter, to help your customer build UAT scripts. They can start building them from the design phase onwards!

Design Presentation

It is important that this presentation is presented at the end of the design phase and that it is at the appropriate level; remember it is a bird's eye view!

Your presentation should cover the following topics:

❏ Introduction – overview of the design, the process used, who was involved, when it took place etc.
❏ Business context – the business landscape surrounding the project and the reason for the project
❏ Process flows – "To Be" scenarios and any proposed business or organisational changes
❏ User requirements – requirements matrix indicating phasing options and sample screens
❏ Technical architecture – high-level overview of technical architecture and summary of implications, for example costs, upgrades etc.
❏ Delivery details – time-frames, costs, teams and technologies
❏ Next steps – steps to move forward, for example sign-off, issue resolution, roles and responsibilities
❏ Issues, assumptions and risks.

Design Must Dos

1. Define design objectives ✓
2. Define design duration ✓
3. Define team and time commitments ✓
4. Prepare your team ✓
5. Create your design schedule ✓
6. Run your design ✓
7. Document and present your findings ✓

1. Define Design Objectives

The main objectives of design are:
❏ To drill into the detail of every single project requirement
❏ To estimate the remaining stages of the project
❏ To finalise the project phasing

- ❏ To design the user interface, i.e. the look and feel of the application
- ❏ To architect the project solution, defining the data, software, hardware and network requirements
- ❏ To define and agree the timeline and project plans for the project implementation
- ❏ To confirm management and user buy-in
- ❏ To prepare the customer and the application for production rollout and ultimately gain acceptance in a production environment.

Figure 10.1: **Key Components and Areas of Focus for Design Phase**

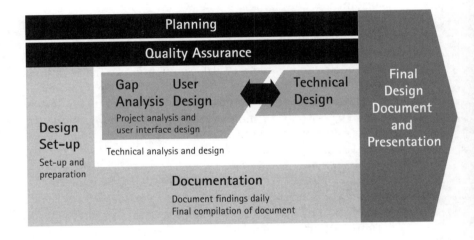

2. Define Design Duration

At the end of the scope you may have committed to a fixed time-frame for the design phase and will probably have built an initial design project plan. You now need to refine this plan to ensure you can meet your deadlines.

Design time can vary from one week to eight weeks, depending upon the requirements, their complexity and customer deadlines. Don't be tempted to cut time from design – it is the foundation of your solution, your blueprint to delivering on time and within budget! And the more time you put into design, the less time you will waste in development.

Plan time for the following:

Area	Tasks
Review time	❑ Scope deliverable (processes, requirements, business case etc.). ❑ Issues, assumptions and risks log and any constraints that may exist.
User design	❑ Estimate the complexity of each group/module of the requirements matrix with a High, Medium or Low rating (H,M,L) – complexity is based upon: — How much is known and not known about the module — How complex the process is — How many screens will be required — How complex the requirement is — How complex the business processes are – will there be a lot of organisational and procedural change? **Rule of thumb estimates are as follows for modules:** ❑ High complexity: 4 days ❑ Medium complexity: 2–3 days ❑ Low complexity: 1 day
Functional components	Complex functionality, such as complex calculation engines, need to be estimated separately and workshops will need to be organised to gather all the rules etc. The time estimates for these depend on the complexity of the functionality you are trying to design.
Technical design	You need to ensure you cover the following topics:

Conceptual architecture	Hardware architecture
Software architecture	Database
Network	Reporting
Connectivity (internal and external)	Error handling
Internationalisation	Performance and concurrency
Operational procedures (batch jobs etc.)	System administration
Security	Manuals, guides etc.
Online help	

Warning: If you are still "designing" during the development phase, the cost of retrofitting solutions is very high. You will have to modify code and re-code completely – a very dangerous scenario.

3. Define Team and Time Commitments

To ensure your design phase is a success you need to involve the right people – the right people from the customer side and the right people that will deliver the project.

Customer Team (all part-time)

- [ ] Visionary – the person who knows what the end result should be.
- [ ] Sponsor – the person who is rubber-stamping the whole project; this can also be the visionary. They will confirm at the end of design that the project is on track and should get the go ahead.
- [ ] Business PM – someone who manages the customer team and coordinates with the delivery team.
- [ ] Business experts – depending on which areas of the business will benefit from the project, there should be a representative from each of these areas. They must also inform the team of other projects that are in progress or are planned that could impact the business solution. They work with the delivery team to review and refine the business flows and review the user interface. They work with the team on functional areas such as calculation engines, providing the rules and algorithms.
- [ ] Users – they work with the delivery team to refine the business flows and create the user interface, i.e. screens and overall look-and-feel of the application.
- [ ] Technologists – the technology experts who provide input into:
  - The customer's current technical landscape
  - The customer's technical strategy for the future
  - Other projects in progress that may impact the technical solution
  - Any other technical information, for example existing agreements with hardware parties etc.

Delivery Team

- ❑ PM – responsible for the delivery of the project (full-time).
- ❑ Business analyst – responsible for the business impact, i.e. process flows and business case (full-time).
- ❑ TL – responsible for the technical solution (full-time).
- ❑ Technical architect – the technical visionary for the entire organisation (part-time).
- ❑ Database administrator – responsible for the data (full-time).
- ❑ Developers – responsible for requirements gathering and documenting (full-time).
- ❑ QA – responsible for reviewing user and technical designs; this can be a peer-to-peer reviewer (part-time).
- ❑ Sales/account manager – responsible for executive client management and escalation of issues (part-time).
- ❑ Finance – review project costs (part-time).

External Roles

During a design phase you may need to interact with external parties to get costs and timelines for particular solutions etc. These could include:

- ❑ Hardware parties
- ❑ Software parties
- ❑ Hosting companies
- ❑ Marketing companies
- ❑ Recruitment companies.

Tip: If you have external parties working with you, make sure your time-frames reflect that fact – they are often not as dedicated to your timelines as you are. Where possible get a fixed time, fixed price contract with them and always ensure they are recognised as a potential risk for your project. They should attend regular checkpoints and meetings and be fully aware of your complete project schedule.

4. Prepare your Team

To prepare for the design phase of a project you will need to:

Area	Tasks
Prepare for design	❏ Build a detailed schedule. ❏ Sort out logistics – location of design, room set-up, lunch requirements etc. ❏ Confirm project understanding and expectations. ❏ Confirm deliverables. ❏ Make contact with external parties (if applicable) – demonstrations, costs etc. ❏ Hold a formal kick-off meeting with customer and delivery team.
Prepare your team	❏ Hold norming session and agree design roles and responsibilities (see Chapter 3). ❏ Review all relevant documentation, e.g. scoping document. ❏ Review customer's current technical landscape – meet with customer's technical group, review technical questionnaire responses. ❏ Review customer's current organisational landscape – meet with business experts in advance. ❏ Research where required, e.g. best-in-class solutions, potential technologies, previous lessons learned etc. ❏ Come up to speed on tools and technologies, e.g. user interface tool. ❏ Arrange training if required and hold training courses if required (internal or external).
Environment set-up	❏ Set up hardware (servers and desktops), network, user accounts etc. ❏ Create design document templates – user, functional, report specifications etc. (see appendices for sample specifications). ❏ Agree any appropriate standards, documentation style, e.g. user interface standards etc.

You need to build a project plan that will cover the development phase through to the rollout phase. This should detail accurate timeframes and resources and needs to outline plans for the following phases:

❏ Development
❏ System testing
❏ Performance testing

❑ UAT
❑ Model office (if required)
❑ Pre-production testing
❑ Project rollout
❑ Support.

In addition agree with the customer who will be carrying out the UAT and provide them with sample UAT scripts and the design document online (once completed) to help them build their own scripts.

5. Create your Design Schedule

Below is a sample eight-week design schedule.

Week 1 Design set-up	Week 2 User design	Week 3 User design	Week 4 User design
❑ Set up design environment ❑ Research and train in appropriate tools ❑ Review all documentation ❑ Review requirements matrix and phasing ❑ Norming ❑ Define roles and responsibilities ❑ Training ❑ Set expectations ❑ Create detailed schedule	❑ Design kick-off ❑ Review scope findings ❑ Define key business scenarios & refine/create business processes ❑ Review requirements matrix in detail ❑ Identify data sources in processes ❑ Define overall screen flows ❑ Identify reporting requirements	❑ Begin screen design ❑ Capture performance expectations ❑ Identify security requirements ❑ Detail functional requirements ❑ Identify connectivity requirements ❑ Create logical database ❑ QA review	❑ Refine screen design ❑ Detail business rules ❑ Update logical database ❑ Create conceptual technical architecture ❑ User checkpoint ❑ Review screen specs ❑ Review requirements specs ❑ Review database ❑ Review issues, risks and assumptions log
Week 5 Technical design	Week 6 Technical design	Week 7 Technical design	Week 8 Documentation
❑ Tools selection process ❑ Network analysis and design ❑ Design h/w & s/w architecture ❑ Design physical DB ❑ Analyse connectivity requirements ❑ Identify system administration requirements ❑ Identify security requirements	❑ Continue h/w & s/w architecture design ❑ Evaluate performance expectations & identify bottlenecks ❑ Design system administration requirements ❑ Continue connectivity design ❑ Continue physical DB design ❑ Identify batch processes and other operational procedures ❑ Perform database sizing ❑ QA review	❑ Finalise h/w & s/w architecture design ❑ Finalise processes design ❑ Finalise database physical schema ❑ Develop pre-production plan ❑ Finalise project plan & create estimations	❑ Document findings ❑ QA document ❑ Provide to customer ❑ Review with customer ❑ Present findings in formal presentation

Tip: While it might not be possible to run workshops for all of your design, you may gather your information via other means, for example one-on-one interviews and or questionnaires. It is important, however, to gather all your team together (customer and delivery) to attend an initial design kick-off meeting and for all prioritisation and phasing exercises to ensure team consensus.

6. Run your Design

The following diagram provides the key areas you need to cover during your design phase.

Figure 10.2: **Key Areas to be Covered During Design Phase**

Project Management

Build design project plan	Identify roles & responsibilities	Develop rollout project plan
Develop user acceptance checklists	Create detailed development project plan	Identify costs, resources and time-frames

Design Set-up	Gap Analysis / User Design	Gap Analysis / Technical Design
❑ Norm	Update business case	Define/agree software architecture
❑ Review business case	Finalise "As Is" processes	Identify 3rd party tools
❑ Understand requirement grouping	Analyse "To Be" processes	Design/modify database
❑ Understand project scope	Requirement identification & grouping	Design systems administration requirements
❑ Review existing systems & constraints	Identify system administration requirements	Define hardware architecture
	Perform data analysis & modelling	Analyse network architecture

Documentation

❑ Project constraints	❑ User interface design
❑ Business case	❑ Database analysis & database design
❑ Requirements matrix	❑ Software & hardware mapping
❑ "To Be" process flows	❑ Software & hardware requirements
❑ Function specifications	❑ Systems management requirements
❑ Algorithm specifications	❑ Preliminary test plan
❑ Report specifications	❑ Development project plan
❑ Screen flows	❑ Project costs

Design Set-Up

This is the opportunity for the team to:

❑ Review all documentation gathered to date, scope document, questionnaires, customer documentation etc.
❑ Research tools, technologies, business
❑ Attend training as required

❏ Set up the design environment, i.e. directory structures, standards (for example GUI standards, document standards etc.), machines, design document templates
❏ Hold a norming session and agree roles and responsibilities
❏ Create and finalise the detailed schedule with your team and your customer.

Gap Analysis/User Design

User design allows the customer to create the look and feel of the new solution. Following the user design sessions, all functionality should have been identified and all user interface screens will have been designed and described in detail. Your user sessions should assess:

❏ The process
❏ The requirements – captured in the requirements matrix
❏ The user interface (for example screens, screen flow, keystrokes etc.)
❏ The functionality supporting the user interface
❏ The data
❏ Security
❏ Performance requirements
❏ System administration.

Gap Analysis/Technical Design

During technical design:

❏ The overall definitive architecture of the solution is created
❏ The complexity for each cell of the requirements matrix is assessed
❏ The technologies and platforms are defined (hardware and software)
❏ The data architecture is created and the database is designed
❏ The points of connectivity are defined and how to connect to each point is investigated and designed
❏ All functions are defined; algorithms should be created where necessary.

A Note on the Technical Specifications

As stated before, the design document is your development blueprint. It is therefore critical that detailed information is captured for every requirement. The following lists the key information required per specification.

Specification Type	Information to Capture During Design
Window	Name Reference (for development environment) Module name (group it belongs to) Description Window layout (actual screen) Database tables used Field tables Event tables Rules Notes Issues Assumptions
Report	Name Reference Description Frequency Users – who requires the report? Selection criteria (parameters for the report) Layout Notes Issues Assumptions
Function	Name Description Parameters Return values Algorithm Notes Issues Assumptions
Connectivity	Interface overview Functional descriptions of the interface Roles & responsibilities (external parties & internal team) Dependencies Notes Issues Assumptions

7. Document and Present your Findings

❑ Create your final document and organise external reviews.
❑ Organise a date for the sponsor presentation – make sure all relevant parties can attend.
❑ Hand out copies of the design document for review.
❑ Agree a date for document feedback.
❑ Agree next steps and assign actions.

It Could Happen to you ...

The Eager Developer

We were in design sessions with a customer on a very tight project schedule. The design was going great, the customer was happy and as we went to look at one particular window, one of the developers piped up, "Do you know what would look cool? Put a tickertape of share prices across the bottom of that window – it's really easy to do too!" This had never been mentioned as a requirement to date; however, the customer thought it would be brilliant. (Note: it didn't add value for the customer, just cool factor!) Nothing could then persuade the customer otherwise.

That requirement was not easy to do – it was a nightmare! It was assigned to the eager developer, following a serious talk after the session about not having bright ideas in front of the clients as agreed in the norming session. After some very late evenings, she came to me and agreed she should have held her tongue when she didn't really know the implications of such a piece of functionality. She did get it done eventually and I'm sure the customer still loves it!

As a PM it is your job to ensure the team understand what is constructive in a working session with a customer – this should be hammered out in the norming session. The developer should have thought of the idea and talked to the PM offline and the idea would have been investigated and definitely put on the back burner – Phase 10 probably!

Appendix 10.1: Sample Window Specification

Introduction
The following documents the details that should be documented in a window specification.

Window Name
Window name as known by the user including requirements matrix cell reference.

Window Reference
A name to reference the window within the development environment.

Module Name
Name of the module associated with the window, referenced from the left-most column in the requirements matrix.

Window Description
A general description of the window, including the following:

- ❏ The purpose of this window
- ❏ How this window is accessed
- ❏ If the screen has more than one mode, for example create and amend, then each of these is described as a separate window.

Window Layout
A picture/screen shot of the window.

Tables Used
The tables used by this window.

Table Name	Purpose
The name of the table in the database.	The use of this table by the screen, e.g. to populate a drop-down, read data or save data.

Field Table
The developer will ultimately use the field table as they are developing the window.

Caption	Required	Data Type	Validation	Data Element Name	Default Value
Name of the field as it appears on the window.	Whether the field is mandatory for input.	The data type of the field.	Validation function or rules for validation on the field. Any notes or special rules that must be applied to this field.	The name of the corresponding field held on the database. Specify table name if ambiguous.	A default value that will be provided by the system.

Grid Table

If there is a grid on the screen then a grid table section is added to the description. The grid table will ultimately be used by the developer as they are developing the window.

Caption	Data Element Name	Notes
Name of the grid column as it appears on the window.	The name of the corresponding field held on the database.	Any additional information required about the grid column.

Event Table

The event table will ultimately be used by the developer as they are developing the functions behind the window.

Description	Function/Operation	Key Sequences	Response
A brief description of the window event. Some examples include: ❑ OK Button Click ❑ File -> Open menu option selected ❑ Text Box Name Lost Focus	Name of the function or class operation invoked by this event. Note that this is not always required.	Any key sequences or control sequences that can be used to activate the action.	Description of the visible changes in the window and/or database occurring as a result of the event and function/operation execution. For example, save the customer information to the database, show a message and clear the data on the current window.

Rules

Any rules specific to the window. This includes user interface and business rules.

Notes

❑ Are there specific relationships between this window and other windows?

❑ What else does the developer need to know?

Issues and Assumptions

❑ What issues are outstanding on this window? What remains to be resolved?

❑ Are there underlying assumptions that this window is based upon?

Appendix 10.2: Sample Functional Specification

The following documents the details that should be documented in a functional specification.

Function Name
The name of the function as it is referred to in the code and the design specification.

Description
The description of the function.

Parameters
The parameters to the function.

Parameter Name	Data Type	Parameter Type	Valid Values/Meaning	Notes
The name of the parameter to the function.	The data type of the parameter.	Input, output or both.	e.g. string	

Return Values
The type of the return value and its possible values.

Data Type	Valid Values	Notes
The data type of the parameter.		

Algorithm
The algorithm used by the function. This description can reference classes or functions/operations defined elsewhere.

Notes
Any notes about the function.

Issues and Assumptions
Any issues or assumptions about the function.

Appendix 10.3: Sample Report Specification

The following outlines the details that should be documented in a report specification:

❑ **Report description** – this gives a general overview of the functionality of each report.
❑ **Frequency** – this section determines when and how often a report will be processed, for example current date, the day the report is being run.
❑ **User(s)** – this section details who requires the report.
❑ **Selection criteria** – the selection criteria outlines the parameters by which the report will be run.
❑ **Report layout** – this describes how the report will be formatted, organised and sorted. This is the most detailed section of the report, giving specific examples of layout and style.
❑ **Issues and assumptions** – this describes any issues or assumptions that affect the report.

Appendix 10.4: Sample Connectivity Specification

The following documents the details that should be documented in a connectivity specification:

❑ **Introduction** – provides a brief introduction of the specific system interface.
❑ **Interface overview** – presents a general description of the interface.
❑ **Functional specifications** – provides detailed information as to what functionality the interface will provide.
❑ **Roles and responsibilities** – identifies the specific party within the external (if an external interface) and internal team that will be responsible for the associated task.
❑ **Dependencies** – lists the requirements that depend on the availability of the associated interface.
❑ **Issues and action items** – lists any outstanding questions/ concerns about the interface and identifies specific tasks that must be completed before the implementation of the interface can begin.
❑ **Assumptions** – lists any assumptions that were made in the design of the interface.

CHAPTER 11

Development

"All project requirements are possible until they have to be done and then the real fun starts!"

Development in a Nutshell

The development phase of your project is the phase where your application is finally created! During this phase you should have very few surprises: the scope of the project should be totally clear and the development blueprint should be detailed in the design document, just needing to be implemented. Each developer gets to build, unit test and integrate their code into the overall application. This is typically the developer's favourite part of the project as they finally get their hands dirty!

It is very important that during the development phase regular checkpoints are organised along with the weekly team and customer meetings. Development can be the longest phase so these checkpoints provide an opportunity for users and management to provide feedback to the delivery team.

The capability of the TL will become extremely obvious during development, as it is during this phase that a good TL will shine and a bad one will cause havoc. The PM must closely monitor that the TL is fulfilling their responsibilities and vice versa – weekly meetings have never been more critical!

Development Deliverables

There are typically three deliverables from a development phase:

1. A working application
2. Supporting documentation:
   - Development document – this is the design document

updated to reflect any changes that occurred during development
  - Issues, risks and assumptions log
  - Testing and rollout plan
  - Test scenarios (produced by users and delivery team)
  - User's guide
  - Programmer's guide
  - System management guide
3. Training documentation – the customer needs to become familiar with the application and learn how to use it, to prepare them for the UAT phase of the project and ultimately rollout.

Development Must Dos

1. Define development objectives ✓
2. Create the project plan ✓
3. Define the team ✓
4. Prepare for development ✓
5. Define the PM responsibilities ✓
6. Organise code reviews ✓
7. Run development testing ✓
8. Arrange the model office ✓
9. Manage change requests ✓
10. Prepare customers for UAT ✓

1. Define Development Objectives

The main objectives of development are:

❑ To build a quality application on time and within budget
❑ To monitor and report on project costs
❑ To manage the change control process
❑ To ensure user buy-in and ownership at the end of development.

The daily development cycle is summarised in Figure 11.1:

Figure 11.1: **Daily Development Cycle**

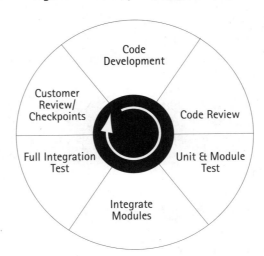

2. Create the Project Plan

At the end of the design phase you should have built your development project plan. You now need to refine this plan to ensure you can meet your deadlines based upon what is now known about:

❑ The project team
  - Their level of experience
  - Their availability – holidays etc.
  - The customer availability
❑ The delivery time-frames or any drop-dead dates
❑ The level of input from third parties, i.e. vendors, partners etc.
❑ The technologies selected in design – is training required?
❑ Hardware availability and delivery schedule
❑ Outstanding issues.

Warning: If your time-frame or budget has been reduced since design, there is often a tendency to throw more resources onto the project. Be careful: adding more people to your team may not always help. You can put multiple people working on a task only if it can be sub-divided. If a task is an autonomous piece of work then only one team member can actually work on it! Always look at dropping functionality as the initial option first. It makes sense after all: "You have shortened my time-frame – what will we drop?"

3. Define the Team

To ensure your development phase is a success you need to involve the right people.

Customer Team (all part-time)

- ❏ Visionary – the person who knows what the end result should be.
- ❏ Sponsor – the person who is rubber-stamping the whole project; this can also be the visionary. They will confirm if the project is on track.
- ❏ Business PM – someone who manages the customer team and coordinates with the delivery team. They usually have the ultimate say on the decision-making process.
- ❏ Business experts – they clarify any issues for the team and may become "super-users", taking part in testing and training other users on the application. They also review the application at checkpoints.
- ❏ Users – a nominated group of super users who review the application and clarify any issues. They participate in UAT and train the rest of the organisation.
- ❏ Technologists – the technology experts who provide input and/or access to:
  - – The customer's existing systems
  - – Other projects in progress that may impact the technical solution
  - – Any other technical information.

Delivery Team

- ❏ PM – responsible for the delivery of a project on time and within budget (full-time).
- ❏ Business analyst – responsible for the business impact of the application, i.e. process flows and business case – will work with the customer team (potentially part-time, depending upon the process changes or new processes to be implemented).
- ❏ TL – responsible for the delivery and quality of the final technical solution (full-time).
- ❏ Technical architect – the technical visionary for the entire organisation – QA of the architecture being implemented (part-time).

❑ Database administrator – responsible for creating the databases, managing the data and interfacing with the developers about access to the data (full-time).
❑ Developers – responsible for developing, documenting and building the application (full-time).
❑ QA – responsible for reviewing standards, for example code reviews, GUI standards etc. This can be a peer-to-peer review once this person is external to the project (part-time).
❑ Sales/account manager – responsible for executive management of the customer and escalation of issues (part-time).
❑ Finance – monitor project costs to date (part-time).

External Parties

During a development phase you may need to work with some external parties that are not directly part of the delivery or customer team. These can include:

❑ Hardware vendors
❑ Software vendors
❑ Hosting companies
❑ Marketing companies
❑ Recruitment companies.

A Note on Working with External Parties

Once external parties are involved in a project its potential risk is increased. In our experience external parties need very strict management: they don't have the same sense of urgency about the project as you do! To mitigate this risk you need to think of them as part of the team. We recommend the following:

❑ Decide upfront who is responsible for managing these external parties – the delivery team PM or the customer team PM?
❑ Invite a representative from all external parties to a development kick-off presentation where you will present the project plan, key milestones and checkpoints.
❑ Invite a representative from all external parties to your weekly customer meeting. They may not need to attend them all, but invite them when needed. You will find they will be more committed to deadlines once they have agreed to them in a meeting environment!

4. Prepare for Development

To prepare for the development phase of a project you will need to focus on the following areas:

Area	Tasks
Team preparation	❑ Organise project staffing and resourcing. ❑ Hold technical review to assess planned architecture and agree standards etc. ❑ Finalise development plan and detail schedule. ❑ Purchase software and/or hardware if required. ❑ Review customer documentation. ❑ Arrange training as required. ❑ Arrange logistics (meeting rooms, supplies, access to customer's site, if not internal). ❑ Hold a development kick-off meeting (internal) – including norming. ❑ Arrange checkpoints with customer. ❑ Arrange checkpoints with external parties. ❑ Arrange weekly status meeting with the customer and external parties. ❑ Arrange weekly meeting with delivery team. ❑ If using a model office, arrange with the customer and agree the process and time-frames.
Environment preparation	❑ Set up hardware. ❑ Install software. ❑ Set up accounts. ❑ Set up communication – network access etc. ❑ Install database. ❑ Arrange additional equipment – projectors, printers etc. ❑ Define directory structures. ❑ Define development standards (for example coding, GUI etc.). ❑ Agree code review time-frames, frequency and expectations. ❑ Arrange connectivity to external sources. ❑ Order production hardware. ❑ Arrange development back-up plan, for example full system back-up carried out each night, source code control etc.

5. Define the PM Responsibilities

As a PM you are responsible for the following throughout the development phase (see Chapter 2 also):

- ❑ Refining the development plan as required on an ongoing basis – as issues arise or get resolved, adjust the project plan to ensure project delivery will be on time. You will need to monitor closely the weekly status meetings and keep both teams updated on the progress of the project
- ❑ Managing the code development process, i.e. code reviews (ensuring they get done) and testing
- ❑ Managing the team
- ❑ Assigning and reviewing documentation tasks – this should be done weekly
- ❑ Enforcing weekly team meetings
- ❑ Enforcing weekly customer meetings and checkpoints
- ❑ Managing the model office if applicable
- ❑ Managing project costs – this includes hardware/software costs and resources (and their associated costs, for example hotel bills, per diems etc.). These costs should be reviewed against the estimated costs to ensure you are within budget
- ❑ Managing issues, risks and assumptions
- ❑ Managing the customer team and ensuring they are managing any associated "organisational change" projects
- ❑ Managing the IT support teams – ensuring the IT support teams receive hardware or software requests in a timely manner.

Development Documentation

The following documents need to be produced during the development phase of a project.

Development document	The design document updated to reflect any changes that occurred during development (Note: should now include error codes and their meanings)
User's guide (if required)	How to use the new application. Typically we recommend that the users write this document, using the design document as its basis
Programmer's guide (if required)	If the application is being handed over to your customer, or your support group, then the support

	team may need a document detailing how to maintain and update the application
System management guide	Explains what needs to be done to keep the application up and running, how to back up the application and how to recover the application (including disaster recovery)
System and user test scenarios	The developers, PM and TL need to build a set of scripts that will test the application end-to-end. It is a set of scripts that test if the application works as required. These tests need to be very detailed and include testing against what was designed in the design document and also negative testing, i.e. tests that try to break the application, for example: you should only be allowed type in characters in Field X; try typing in numbers and see what happens! (See Testing, Chapter 12.)

6. Organise Code Reviews

It is important that the PM ensures that the TL has made it clear what is expected of the developers when they are coding and testing. The TL should provide each team member with the set of coding standards at the start of the development phase in the norming session. The goal of coding standards is to ensure that the entire set of source code looks consistent and can be read and maintained by any member of the team, not just the developer who wrote it!

It is important that:

- ❑ Coding standards are defined before the start of development – it is extremely challenging and dangerous to retrofit standards on code and try to deliver your project on time
- ❑ Coding standards are concise – be sensible, not everything needs to be standardised – the developers will only remember a realistic amount
- ❑ Developers understand the purpose and criticality of following these standards and buy into them
- ❑ Where possible an independent QA person should deliver the coding standards and enforce them during code reviews. If a QA person is not available the TL must assume this role!

See Appendix 11.1 and 11.2 for sample unit interface and for functions.

Code Reviews

When development begins, the TL must hold formal code reviews to ensure the developers are adhering to the standards and to identify any renegade programmers!

We recommend the following:

- ❑ Begin code reviews early in the project – to catch issues upfront
- ❑ Allow one day (two half days) for each code review – do a few during the project
- ❑ Ensure you have identified time in your project plan for technical reviews, code reviews and for the suggested code modifications to be implemented and re-reviewed
- ❑ Update your coding standards following the review if appropriate and re-distribute
- ❑ Create a list of "typical coding issues" and distribute it to the team.

Why Do Code Reviews?

- ❑ They are critical for QA purposes – they ensure a quality deliverable.
- ❑ They provide a key learning opportunity – through the formal code review process junior and senior developers get to work together and see other people's code: the senior developers can identify bugs and help the junior developers with suggested fixes or improvements and the junior developers can read and learn about more complex code. The TL can also identify strong and weak developers.
- ❑ They provide an opportunity for the group to challenge current methods and potentially introduce new methodologies or standards.

Code Review Process

The following details the process we recommend for doing code reviews.

	Code Review Process
Gather code samples and distribute	❑ Each team member provides a sample of code to the code review coordinator (either an external QA person or the TL). The developer remains anonymous.

	❑ The coordinator amalgamates the code samples into a document and distributes it to the entire team for review. ❑ The coordinator also provides the developers with a copy of the coding standards and typical issues to look for.
Prepare feedback	❑ Each team member reviews the code samples and prepares their comments and feedback.
Hold a review meeting	❑ The coordinator facilitates a session where all code samples are assessed and the team provide all of their comments and feedback. ❑ The feedback is discussed and recommended changes are provided.
Provide a report on the findings	The coordinator provides a report back to the team, detailing: ❑ What was reviewed ❑ Common issues ❑ Fixes to be made ❑ Modifications to the coding standards, if any.
Follow–up	❑ The developers implement the changes, unit test the code and the changes are reviewed by the coordinator to ensure the review was understood.

The following details some sample topics to focus on in a code review:

What to Look for in a Code Review

❑ Input/output requirements
❑ Clean-up and housekeeping
❑ Exit conditions
❑ Source code quality – understanding and maintainability
   – Comments
   – Formatting
   – Variable names
   – Hard-coded variables
   – Degree of complexity allowed, e.g. how many nested loops you can have
   – Maximum number of routines in a class/module (if applicable)
❑ Adherence to coding standards
❑ Performance issues
❑ User interface standards
❑ Temporary file clean-up

❏   Environment independence
❏   Naming conventions for source code files
❏   Memory usage
❏   Exception handling
❏   Security issues
❏   Recovery

7. Run Development Testing

To get your application ready for the formal testing phase, your developers will need to code and test all of the following key areas of development.

Key Application Development Areas
❏   User interface, i.e. screen development
❏   Functions
❏   Connectivity interfaces
❏   Classes (if applicable)
❏   Database and associated functionality (stored procedures etc.)
❏   Reports
❏   Data migration scripts
❏   Security
❏   User administration and maintenance
❏   System administration (back-up, recovery etc.)

While a formal test phase will follow the development phase testing begins in development with the smallest unit of code! You should ensure that your team know exactly what is expected of them by training and preparing them. There are three key test areas to plan for in your development phase:

1. Unit testing
2. Component/module testing
3. Integration testing.

The following sections briefly explain each one of these to give you a basic understanding of what should be involved. For each we have outlined a brief summary. Where possible we have included some sample checklists. However, due to the nature of varying solutions, you will need to work very closely with the TL to plan their implementation in detail. Remember, each phase requires some planning and preparation.

Unit Testing Summary

- ✓ Is continuous during the development – it should be noted that unit testing is *part* of the development effort and should be included when estimating a development effort for each piece of functionality.
- ✓ Is testing of source code by the developer who wrote it.
- ✓ Typically applies to screens, functions, subroutines, modules and classes.
- ✓ Must be done before it is integrated with other source code.
- ✓ Unit test uses "white box" testing technique (see Testing, Chapter 12).
- ✓ Must be tested and documented by developer and formally signed off by TL.

The Top Ten Unit Test Checks

1. Documentation is accurate and complete.
2. Functional overview is complete.
3. All issues that have potential functional impact have been resolved.
4. All issues identified during the code review process have been implemented and tested.
5. All coding standards have been incorporated.
6. Unit testing has been completed for:
   - Functionality
   - User Interface (UI).
7. All existing bugs and UI issues have been resolved.
8. Unit test documentation has been updated to include necessary bug fixes and signed by TL.
9. Performance is consistent with established performance requirements.
10. The final version of the program files has been placed on the network in your source code control system.

Module/Component Testing Summary

☑ Staggered during development phase – allow checkpoints in your plan for this.

☑ Performed to confirm the data flows correctly through the integrated units and that the integrated units meet the design requirements.

☑ This stage of testing should include tests designed to catch memory leaks and possibly early performance bottlenecks.

☑ Tested by PM, QA, TL and developers, formally signed off by TL.

How Ready Are you for Module Testing?

Module testing should not begin until the module meets the following criteria:

❑ Module test plan and schedule is complete
❑ Team training on module testing is done
❑ Unit testing is complete, the unit test checklists have been signed off and passed by the TL
❑ The units/screens meet the required criteria, for example all "critical" and "high" bugs are fixed, the units/screens are regression tested and all code is frozen
❑ Build and release process is developed and tested for both the modules and the database, and is stable and reliable (release forward/rollback); a "smoke" test suite has been defined
❑ All test scripts/drivers are complete and tested
❑ Module test environment is ready
❑ Test data set is complete (accurate and sufficient volume)
❑ Test data and other supporting software are loaded.

When Are you Finished Module Testing?

In order to start integration testing, the module testing process should pass the following criteria:

❑ The module has successfully completed two passes of module testing
❑ There has been a final code freeze and every module has been successfully regression tested after the code-freeze

- [ ] No outstanding "critical" or "high" bugs (unless approved by PM or TL)
- [ ] All modules have received at least two hours of random black-box testing where possible
- [ ] Functionality of module meets design requirements
- [ ] All screens within the module have been through usability testing
- [ ] Design document update is complete.

A Note on Code Freezing

When all development is completed and all the units have been successfully unit tested there should be a code freeze meeting in order to determine if the code is ready to be frozen. A code freeze implies that no new functionality will be added – the only changes to the code from now on will be as a result of bug fixing. The PM, TL, QA lead, developers and representatives from the user team should attend this meeting. The meeting should be coordinated by the PM. Any changes must be negotiated as enhancements.

Deliverables

- [ ] Units of software fully tested and integrated with all other units within a module.
- [ ] Module test summary report from bug-tracking database.
- [ ] Integration test plan and schedule.
- [ ] Integration scenarios (including test scripts/drivers).
- [ ] Test environment that meets integration test requirements (including test data and other supporting software).
- [ ] First draft of system test plan (required towards end of development).
- [ ] First draft of user scenarios (required towards end of development).

Integration Testing Summary

- [x] Staggered during development, testing of interaction between multiple modules in the system.
- [x] Confirms that data flows between the integrated modules and the modules function correctly.
- [x] Confirms integrated modules match the design specification.
- [x] May identify performance issues early – prior to system test.
- [x] Tested by PM, QA, TL and developers, formally signed off by TL.

How Ready Are you for Integration Testing?

❑ Integration test plan and schedule is complete.

❑ Team training focusing on integration testing is done.

❑ Module testing is complete, the module checklists have been signed off and passed.

❑ All "critical" and "high" bugs are fixed, the modules are regression tested.

❑ Modules pass the smoke test.

❑ Integration test environment is ready.

❑ Test data set is complete (accurate, clean and sufficient volume).

❑ Test data and other supporting software are loaded.

When Are you Finished Integration Testing?

In order to start system testing, the integration testing process should pass the following criteria:

❑ All integrated modules have successfully completed two passes of integration testing

❑ All integrated modules have been regression tested at least twice

❑ No outstanding "critical" or "high" bugs (unless approved by PM or TL)

❑ All integrated modules have received at least two hours of random black-box testing where possible

❑ Functionality of integrated modules meets design requirements

❑ Design document update is complete.

Deliverables

❑ All integrated modules have been approved and signed off by TL.

❑ Integration test summary report from bug-tracking database.

❑ Finalised system test plan and schedule.

❑ Confirmed and reviewed user scenarios.

❑ Documented test scripts/drivers.

❑ Test environment checklist which meets system test requirements (including test data and other supporting software).

❑ System test kick-off presentation for delivery team and customers.

Warning: It is very inefficient and expensive to send unstable and unprepared software into the next phase at any stage of testing. If the testing criteria cannot be met, the software should stay in the current testing phase until it can pass the criteria and is ready for the next level of testing.

8. Arrange the Model Office

The model office is a separate environment that is typically set up and manned by super users, for users during a long development phase. The model office plays a critical part in the acceptance and verification of a new application within an organisation. If you are implementing a new system that will significantly impact your users it is best to plan for a model office. The model office is a simulated application environment that can demonstrate: the new application, new or changed business processes, new procedures and new technologies. While the delivery PM is responsible for ensuring it happens, the super users should own and run the model office. We recommend the following for setting up a formal model office environment:

❑ Set up a separate, easily accessible room with four to five PCs – man it with one to two super users (who know the application inside out), decorate it with posters explaining new processes, new technologies, new roles etc.

❑ Run model office shows – create a schedule of shows to run a presentation and demonstration of the new application. Create a rota of users to attend each day. Allow users access to PCs so they can run the demo themselves if required.

❑ Provide a comments box to feed back to the development team – assess all feedback, arrange a formal meeting with the delivery and customer team. Incorporate changes where feasible and give feedback at the next model office event, for example "Mary suggested we add a field for directions, as you can see it's in!"

❑ In a six-month development there should be at least four model office events, which should coincide with integration milestones.

❑ Allow one to two days in the project plan for every model office event for the delivery team to create the demo.

 **Warning:** We have seen model office environments where slices of actual code are released into the environment to allow users actually "play" with the application. We do not recommend this in the development phase, as there is a risk of many bugs arising and it can annoy users! At this stage we recommend using an automated recording tool to record a few sample user scenarios. Remember, the key purpose of a model office is to prepare the users for acceptance. A good UAT phase will also play a major role in acceptance of a new application.

9. Manage Change Requests

Managing the changes that are requested by users/management after the design is complete can be a very difficult task. If it is not managed correctly it will cause "scope creep" and your project will never deliver on time or within budget.

To control "scope creep" and manage these changes, you as a PM must educate your team, your users and your customers on the process that they must follow if they have a change that is not part of the original design. The recommended process is as follows:

Change Request Process
❏ User must document all change requests no matter how small (see a sample change request form in Chapter 12). They must refer back to the design document and explain why they need this change.
❏ The change request form must go through the PM. This ensures you control what changes are being requested.
❏ The PM and TL must assess requests and categorise them based upon impact, i.e.:   — Impact upon business process   — Impact on design/development – all aspects of technical impact, for example screens, database, batch jobs, reports, performance etc.   — Impact upon development time-frames   — Impact on budget.
❏ Document your findings on each request and make the executive sponsor make the call if it is anything that will affect project delivery date and budget.
❏ The request is either accepted or declined – hold a meeting with requestor to inform them.
❏ If request is accepted, design each change.

10. Prepare Customers for UAT

Typically your customer has a number of responsibilities on your project. One key responsibility is to create the UAT scripts. These scripts should test all aspects of the application, from the screens to the batch jobs, to system recovery etc. Often the PM provides the system test scripts as a basis for the UAT scripts, to give the customer a head start. Make sure the user team understands that following UAT they will be signing off the application, so they must ensure they have tested sufficiently to confidently sign off the application.

The users may also need to become familiar with the application and may need time with some of your developers to become familiar with the overall application. It is important that super users are trained; it is then their responsibility to train the rest of the users. Try not to use your developers to train users. The PM can help with the training schedule, handbook etc. but it is best if the super-user team train the rest of the organisation.

It Could Happen to you ...

The Developer that Wasn't!

There was a project I reviewed where I was playing a QA role and the following situation occurred: There was a developer who had absolutely no idea how to develop – how was he hired, who knows? He was developing part of the user interface of the application. Some time into the project, the TL noticed that the performance of the application was very slow and decided to have a code review with the team to see if it could shed any light on the issue. It emerged from the code review that this developer was causing the problem.

On this project if a developer needed to pass a piece of data from a window to a function, they would pass just the piece of data, a string or a number for example. Not this developer! He decided the easiest thing to do was pass a copy of the entire window and access the data from within that copy of the window. These windows were huge and of course were making the application grind to a halt. The developer was "hastily educated" and practically all the code he had developed was rewritten.

Luckily the code review happened early on in the project or the cost and time for restructuring all that code would have been enormous. Remember two things: hold your code reviews early and often and always test the skills of your developers!

• •

Appendix 11.1: **Sample Unit Test Criteria for a User Interface**

Overall Layout

❏   Does the screen reflect all of the functionality specified in the requirements document?

❏   Is the screen easy to understand, learn, use?

❏   Does the screen layout match the user's process?

❏   Is the default button appropriate during the dialog interaction?

❏   For dialog boxes – are push buttons placed at correct part of the screen and aligned correctly?

❏   Are push buttons ordered correctly and are they consistent with other screens?

❏   Are push buttons/fields/etc. aligned top/bottom/left/right appropriately?

❏   Do all entry/text field labels end with a colon (:)?

❏   Do all other text labels (check box, group box, list box) not end with a colon (:)?

❏   Are all text labels left aligned with other labels positioned above or below?

❏   Has the correct default push button been selected and is it activated when Enter is pressed?

❏   Has entry-field validation been included for all required fields?

Screens

❏   Make sure all "Drop Down" fields are sorted either alphabetically or otherwise.

❏   Verify all Default fields on all screens.

❏   Is dialog window title consistent with the button on the calling dialog?

❏   Are default values set properly?

❏   Are the default values the best choices for defaults in terms of common usage?

❏   Is the cursor initially placed in the correct control or position within a control (tab order)?

❏   Is the default window placement and size correct?

❏   Is the layout and spacing consistent?

❏   Is the purpose of buttons clear and consistent?

❏   Is it clear which controls are affected by which buttons? (place buttons near appropriate controls)

❏   Does the window have a standard background?

❏   Do push buttons, text fields and labels have standard colours and size?

❏   Do disabled push buttons appear disabled (grayed)?

❏   Does the dialog box have the correct modality (pop-up windows should be modal)?

❏   Is the standard font being used for all text?

Functional Working of the User Interface

❑ Are controls appropriately enabled/disabled based on "state" of screen?
❑ Does entry-field validation work correctly for all required fields?
❑ Can windows be minimised, maximised, restored, moved, sized, closed where applicable?
❑ Do modal dialog windows NOT have minimise and maximise buttons?
❑ Do screens correctly behave as part of their parent window (i.e. should not be able to move windows outside parent)?
❑ Are windows displayed in the correct size and position (not obscuring title bar of previous window)?

User/Warning/Error Messages

❑ Is message text formatted correctly in the message box?
❑ Are messages phrased in a standard way?
❑ Is message wording understandable and clear?
❑ Do messages indicate further action for the user to take if necessary to complete a task?
❑ Does error message text use full stops instead of exclamation marks?
❑ Is the message title appropriate (error/warning)?
❑ Is the message icon appropriate?
❑ Is cursor placed correctly after the error message is closed?
❑ Is message text grammar and spelling correct?
❑ If messages have error severity levels, is the correct colour, icon, etc. displayed for that message?
❑ Are the messages stored in the appropriate place in the database?

Wording

❑ Is upper and lower case used appropriately?
❑ Will abbreviations be understood?
❑ Is all spelling correct?
❑ Are all words necessary?
❑ Do buttons that bring up dialogs contain ellipses (...)?
❑ Is wording clear and easy to understand?

Keyboard Navigation

❑ Can you tab through all controls?
❑ Is the tabbing order logical and correct?
❑ Does Shift-Tab work correctly to tab in reverse order?
❑ Do all editable controls have accelerators?
❑ Do accelerator keys select appropriate controls?

❑   Are accelerator keys unique?
❑   Can the window be used to carry out intended usage using keyboard only?
❑   Can the window be used to carry out intended usage using mouse only?

Performance

❑   Are the events happening fast enough?
❑   Are you clear if the system is processing your request or waiting for your input?
❑   Is there appropriate graphical feedback when the system is processing?
❑   Is there appropriate textual feedback (status messages) when the system is processing?

Appendix 11.2: Sample Unit Test Criteria for Functions

Each function in the module executes correctly. ❑ All paths within the function execute correctly. ❑ The function is invoked correctly, in every way that the function can be invoked. ❑ All data formatting is correct.	All functions that interact with other modules are correct, and data inputs/outputs are correct.
All paths within a module, i.e. inter-function interactions, execute correctly.	Intended user scenarios work correctly and data is correct.
All outputs to file are correct.	Low disk space conditions have been tested for any functions which write to the server or local workstation disk: ❑ Ensure that an error message instructs to free up disk space ❑ If appropriate, the error message should indicate that data may be lost.
Status messages are correct and are displayed at appropriate times.	Hourglass is displayed at appropriate times.
Messages display for the appropriate condition(s): ❑ Usage messages ❑ Warning messages ❑ Error messages.	System error conditions appropriately handled.
Database error conditions correctly handled	**Numeric Fields** All numeric fields have been tested with input which could be specified by the user and are correctly handled (smallest, largest, negative etc.).
Date Fields All date fields have been tested for and are correctly handled, e.g.: ❑ Feb. 29 in a leap year ❑ Feb. 29 in a non-leap year ❑ Nonsense dates ❑ The year 0 ❑ Negative year ❑ Empty field ❑ Values which use the minimum field length ❑ Values which use the maximum field length.	**Character Fields** All character fields have been tested for and are correctly handled: ❑ Typical character entries ❑ Blanks in entry text ❑ No blanks in entry text ❑ All blanks ❑ Empty field ❑ Null characters ❑ Numbers ❑ Non-letter characters (i.e.: $ # % & ") ❑ Values which use the minimum field length ❑ Values which use the maximum field length.

Testing

Software Testing in a Nutshell

Testing is the measurement of quality of your project. It is the most dangerous and underestimated phase of every project. As a PM you must measure how closely you have achieved quality by testing areas such as reliability, usability, maintainability, compatibility, sustainability and reusability.

Testing must be viewed as an integral part of any software development project – it takes place as a continual assessment of whether the software being produced will meet the needs of the users. It begins at the design phase. With this in mind, it is important to base all testing activities on the business and user needs, objectives, processes and scenarios. A "zero bug" system that does not meet business requirements is not a success.

Errors/defects/bugs, we'll call them bugs, will occur! This is because project teams are human and teams are usually working under resource, time and technology constraints. Absolute exhaustive testing would in most cases take an enormous amount of resources and is therefore usually impractical. However, to test your project thoroughly you will need to focus on the following key areas:

1. The People	2. The Environment	3. The Techniques
❏ Team	❏ Development	❏ White box
❏ Support structures	❏ Pre-production	❏ Black box
	❏ Production	❏ Random black box
		❏ Regression/verification
		❏ Smoke/pre-release
		❏ Automated
4. The Phases	**5. The Process**	**6. The Testing Tools**
❏ Unit	❏ Bug tracking	❏ CAST (computer
❏ Component		aided software tools)
❏ Integration		❏ Tool selection
❏ System		
❏ Performance		
❏ UAT		
❏ Production and rollout		

This chapter aims to highlight the key areas of testing at a high level only. Testing is the one area of an IT project that will require detailed planning tools and tests to ensure a quality result.

Where to Start?

A PM should be preparing for the testing phase during the development phase of a project. Once development has been completed and signed off the team then needs to get prepared too.

The process begins by holding a testing kick-off meeting:

- ✓ Prepare your team – allow at least two days' team preparation before any formal testing begins. Remember, at this stage it is assumed that all unit test and module testing has been completed and signed off
- ✓ Norm your team (see Chapter 3)
- ✓ Define testing roles and responsibilities for each team member
- ✓ Present a testing overview: testing plan, deliverables for each phase, time-frames
- ✓ Define testing standards and methodology
- ✓ Gather and prepare all testing documentation to be used
- ✓ Demonstrate any tools you will be using, for example bug tracking, automation
- ✓ Agree deliverables for every testing phase with your team and customer
- ✓ Discuss concerns or worries with your team
- ✓ Define project administration:
  - Back-up, security, documentation, checking in/out procedures.

You then need to prepare your users/testers:

- ❑ Start the testing phase with a kick-off presentation explaining what to test and how to test
- ❑ Agree schedules and time commitments
- ❑ Explain the test environment
- ❑ Discuss the testing methodology to be used
- ❑ Present tool, documents, daily reports to be used, for example change requests, bug-tracking database, status reports

❑ Set expectations for testing – testing is very frustrating for users, they will find bugs, that's their job. Manage your users very carefully – you don't want bad PR at this stage
❑ Review their test scenarios; document and divide out scenarios
❑ Define bug ratings, i.e. high, low, cosmetic, enhancement
❑ Open a bug book on the total bug count – this adds a bit of fun – give a bottle of champagne for the closest estimate!

Then prepare for everything else:

❑ Ensure system test room/environment is set up and that the test machines configuration is complete
❑ Ensure test data set is complete (accurate, sufficient volume)
❑ Define data-gathering process and responsibilities
❑ Ensure test data and other supporting software are loaded on all test machines
❑ Define procedures for general troubleshooting and escalation of issues
❑ Ensure the support and user teams begin to understand that they must now begin to take ownership of the system.

Testing Documents

You need to produce a number of documents in advance of the testing phase:

✓ Updated development document (which was the design document updated during development)
✓ Test plans for all major test phases, i.e.
  – System test
  – Performance and concurrency test
  – UAT
  – Production Acceptance Test (PAT)
✓ User scenarios – created by your users
✓ Bug-reporting form
✓ Change request form
✓ User acceptance form
✓ Bug-tracking database reports
✓ Installation manual

✓ Back-up and recovery guidelines (including all manual procedures)
✓ Administration manual
✓ Performance guidelines
✓ Rollout activities checklist.

The formal test document (test plan) for each of the major test phases is required; this ensures buy-in and a clear guide on how you will run each phase. The test plan should cover the following topics:

✓ Introduction – overview of the test phase, kick-off meeting, when, where, how long, who is involved, expectations
✓ Test objectives
✓ Roles and responsibilities
✓ Time-frames – a schedule for the duration
✓ Readiness checklist
✓ Planning and communication – what meetings you will have during the phase?
✓ Test environment – environment set-up checklist, hardware, software, data requirements
✓ Test data – when, how and who gets it
✓ Testing methodology and techniques
✓ Test areas – what is to be tested?
✓ Testing assumptions and dependencies
✓ Graduation criteria
✓ Deliverables
✓ Sign-off form.

Setting the Performance Guidelines

Before testing commences you and your team must understand the performance expectations of your users/customers. You should create a table like the following and agree performance expectations for each major module of the application before testing commences. Establish performance guidelines for normal conditions, peak conditions, partial system failure and scalability. These guidelines will be used as benchmark figures during system and production acceptance testing.

Performance Rating	Criteria
1	Excellent (Immediate)
2	Acceptable (< 5 seconds)
3	Poor (10–20 Seconds)
4	Unacceptable (> 30 seconds)

The Main Testing Components

The following table represents the major testing components that a PM needs to focus on to ensure all critical aspects of testing are covered:

1. The People	2. The Environment	3. The Testing Techniques
❏ Team ❏ Support structures	❏ Development ❏ Pre-production ❏ Production	❏ White box ❏ Black box ❏ Random black box ❏ Regression/verification ❏ Smoke/pre-release ❏ Automated
4. The Phases	**5. The Process**	**6. The Testing Tools**

❏ Unit
❏ Component
❏ Integration
❏ System
❏ Performance
❏ UAT
❏ Production and
  rollout
	❏ Bug tracking	❏ CAST (computer aided
		  software tools)
		❏ Tool selection

1. The People

Testing Roles

The following full-time testing roles should be assigned when you reach the end of the development phase of your project (Note: people can take on multiple roles):

☑ PM – responsible for the overall methodology and quality of the testing phase; must have the ability to be a brilliant tester!

- ✓ TL – responsible for technical quality and excellence, coding standards and performance implications, manages and supports the technical team
- ✓ Developers/fixers – develop and fix the code and responsible for all unit testing, fixes to the code and document updates
- ✓ Release manager – responsible for releasing a version of code for general testing, typically the TL or a very senior developer can assume this role
- ✓ QA lead – responsible for implementing best practice test procedures, quality test scripts and managing the scheduling of the testers. The PM can assume this role
- ✓ Users/testers – responsible for writing test case scenarios, testing and sign-off
- ✓ DBA – play a major role in ensuring data are loaded and clean for all the different environments in all phases
- ✓ IT support – responsible for the test environments and hardware set-up.

Team Responsibilities

The following table is a very good guide on the types of tasks that arise in the testing phases. It is a very handy tool to use in a norming session to divide out responsibilities among the team. Additional tasks can be added based upon your project type.

Tasks	PM	TL	QA	Developers Lead	Users	IT	DBA Support	Business Analyst
Organise your customer re having test scenarios and test data ready								
Provide user scenarios and test/production data to the team								
Define bug-fixing process								
Define bug-reporting process								
Set up bug-tracking and QA database								
Research and identify								

testing tools								
Set up hardware and software								
Set up/update/maintain testing environments								
Define performance requirements								
Ensure all appropriate tools are loaded and configured								
Ensure the test data is loaded								
Verify that test data set is complete								
Create database scripts to reset data to initial state								
Create application build and release procedure								
Create change request process								
Determine application acceptance criteria								
Define testing standards								
Manage testing process (schedule and resources)								
Monitor and update schedule								
Assign resources (bug fixers/testers)								
Provide status reports to customer								
Create testing reports								
Run build and release process								
Build executable								
Release latest version								
"Smoke" test executable								
Documentation								
Update design document								
Update test plans and								

templates									
Update test cases									
Update project plan									
Manage UAT plan creation									
Review and approve test plans and scenarios									
Prepare UAT acceptance letter									
Define team structure									
Logistics – set up UAT room and equipment									
Set up test environment for pre-release testing									
Define pre-release test scenarios									
Identify key customer resources									
Train customer resources									
Establish daily goals for developers									
Establish daily goals for testers									
Test/identify and report bugs/verify fixes									
Assign bugs to developers									
Change priority of bugs									
Fix bugs/unit test code									
Pre-release/regression testing									
Update PM on effort of unresolved bug fixes									

2. The Environment

One area that you need to define clearly is your testing and production environments. For each testing phase there should be one or more separate environments set up. Typically associated with each environment is:

✓ The physical machine where the environment resides, and associated network and storage infrastructure

- ✓ Additional security deployments, for example encryption
- ✓ and user groups and names
- ✓ The database
- ✓ The dataset
- ✓ Any relevant files, for example scripts, batch jobs, configuration settings etc.
- ✓ The directory set-up
- ✓ The application
- ✓ Depending on the environment there may be different software items needed, for example when unit testing in the development environment you need appropriate testing and debugging tools, access to bug tracking software etc.

We recommend that where possible you have a separate development and production server. This will ensure that the development environments will not impact on your production system. It is important too from a failover perspective – if your production server goes down, you will have a back-up server available to keep your application live. Of course, it is not always feasible to have two servers and if you don't then partition your server into development and production "virtual" machines.

Warning: It is critical that all organisations have a disaster recovery plan in place for all existing systems and applications. Most organisations put this to the back of the queue to create, test and rollout. Remember, however, that if a disaster occurs the recovery plan could be the making or breaking of your organisation! You need to get buy-in from the top management and then the entire organisation and implement. Once you have buy-in, implement the plan.

The following table shows the set of environments typically required for the delivery of an IT project and the related testing associated with each environment. Depending upon your project and the complexity of the application you may not need all environments but you certainly should seriously discuss the value of them all before omitting any!

Recommended Environments	Related Testing	Description
Development	Unit Component Integration	**Development phase** Used by the delivery team for developing and fixing bugs during unit, component and integration testing.
System test	Integration System	**System test phase** Used by the delivery team to test the application before it is released into the UAT environment. The configuration of the system test environment is a copy of the latest development environment configuration.
Performance and concurrency	Performance and concurrency	**All phases** This environment is typically used during the system testing phase and the pre-production phase. Volumes of data need to be loaded and manipulated for extreme testing!
UAT Note: None of the development environment tools, debuggers, compilers, etc. should be present on the users' test machines.	UAT	**UAT phase** Used by users for running the user scenarios. This UAT environment configuration should replicate the planned production environment configuration, showing "real data", and should be refreshed daily.
Training	N/A	**UAT and pre-production phase** Used by super users to train the rest of the organisation. The training environment configuration is a copy of the production environment configuration, including associated production data.
Pre-production (Pre-prod)	Pre-prod Performance and concurrency	**Rollout phase** Used to test the application prior to release into production. The pre-prod environment configuration is a replica of the production environment configuration.

Production environment	Production	**Production phase** The environment that supports the live application; contains all the production data.

The following diagram summarises the recommended environments you need to plan for during the delivery of an IT project:

Figure 12.1: Environments and Associated Testing Phases

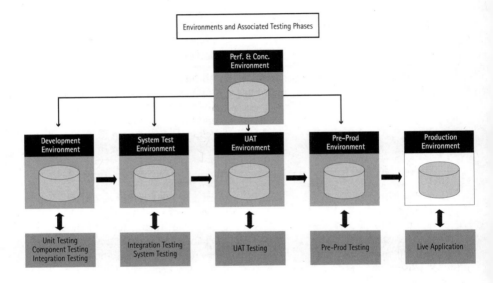

Warning: Data requirements need a lot of planning and usually more scrubbing than often expected. Invariably, project teams have found they underestimate both the effort and time that will be required to get data (both legacy and newly created) ready for use. Ideally, you want to be able to start using customer data as early as integration testing. Data planning should begin during the design phase. Make sure there are milestones in the project plan for early data loads. For medium to large projects always ensure you have a dedicated DBA role.

Release Procedures

Every organisation needs to define a set of release procedures, to release the application from development through to production. It is so important for the integrity of your application that this procedure is clearly defined and understood by all relevant parties. If code is put into production incorrectly there can be very serious consequences.

A Note on Environment Ownership

When delivery, support and IT services teams co-exist in an organisation, division of responsibilities can become unclear. To make it easier we recommend the following:

- ✓ From design phase onwards representative(s) from all peripheral support teams should become part of the delivery team on a part-time basis. They should be invited to meetings at the design stage. Ideally a member of the support team should become a co-developer with minimum functionality to develop. In this way the support team get to know the application in the early stages.

- ✓ An application or project is "owned" by the delivery team until it passes the UAT phase and reaches the pre-production phase, where responsibility is handed over to the support team, though members of the delivery team are available for an agreed amount of time to continue support.

- ✓ The delivery team is responsible for all test phases up to and during UAT. The support team take over for pre-production and production testing.

- ✓ The support team is responsible for the production environment.

- ✓ All relevant documentation, i.e. installation manuals, back-up and recovery manuals, manual procedures, database dictionaries etc., are completed by the delivery team (in conjunction with the support team) and handed over to the support team at the end of the UAT phase.

- ✓ The delivery team should issue environment checklists to the technical services teams well in advance of the testing phases. The technical services team is responsible for setting up the test environments along with the DBA.

• •

Warning: Don't forget about the physical environments. For example, will UAT take place in a separate room, building or even country to the delivery team? This will have several implications that must be considered, such as server requirements, PC set-up, release procedures, bug monitoring and training. Setting up a clean UAT environment is critical and it demands a lot of time and good management.

3. The Testing Techniques

During all phases of testing, you should ensure that various testing techniques are applied. The most well-known testing techniques can be summarised as follows:

- ❑ White box – also known as glass box, structural, clear box and open box
- ❑ Black box
- ❑ Data integrity
- ❑ Random black box also known as "error guessing" or "bang away"!
- ❑ Regression also known as verification
- ❑ Smoke also known as pre-release
- ❑ Automated.

Testing Techniques in Summary

White Box	Black Box
❑ Typically used in development for unit and integration testing. ❑ Tester requires explicit knowledge of the internal workings of the code being tested to select the test data. ❑ Unlike black-box testing, white-box testing uses specific knowledge of programming code to examine outputs. ❑ The test is accurate only if the tester knows what the program is supposed to do and can see if the	❑ Carried out by another person, i.e. not the original developer – the internal workings of the code being tested are not known by the tester. ❑ The tester only knows the inputs and the expected outcomes – based upon external interactions only. ❑ The tester only needs to know what the design specification is and the testing is based upon carefully controlled scenario

program diverges from its intended goal.

❑ White box testing does not account for errors caused by omission of sections of the user specifications.

testing of each functional area, using pre-planned input and checking expected outcomes.

Data-Integrity Testing	**Random Black Box**
❑ Aimed at ensuring the data that is presented by the system is consistent with the database. ❑ It is desirable that the exact data being entered in the test scenarios is known beforehand in order to give the testers information for checking the integrity of the data. ❑ Tester looks for bugs such as date fields displaying incorrectly, numeric data appearing in text fields and vice versa, incorrect date formats, incorrect calculations etc.	❑ Ensure the PM, QA, TL or non-developer does this testing. A PM should aim to do this at least once a day; be ruthless but sympathetic to the stage you are at. ❑ Testers use experience and intuition of where errors have occurred in the past and are likely to occur in the future (e.g. 30 February). ❑ This technique is less structured and less formal; however, it allows the tester greater freedom to input and scrutinise results in an attempt to "break" the system. It is used to supplement the other systematic testing that occurs. ❑ Allows the tester freedom to "bang away" on the system and try to "break" the system. ❑ If bugs are found, the tester must document the scenario tested, detail the bug found and ultimately re-test before sign-off.
Regression	**Smoke**
❑ The selective retesting of a system that has been modified to ensure that the bug correction/modification does not cause other aspects of the program or system to regress, thereby introducing new errors, i.e. that: – Any bugs that have been fixed are working – No other previously working	❑ A relatively simple test process to check whether the software "smokes" or breaks when it is run (originates from electrical engineering – a test to check whether an electrical device actually smokes when it is switched on!). ❑ The smoke test is not an exhaustive test; it just covers basic functionality, but must cover enough of the

functions have failed as a result of the fixes

— Newly added features have not created problems with previous versions of the software.

❑ It is a quality control measure to ensure that the newly modified code still complies with its specified requirements and that unmodified code has not been affected by the maintenance/upgrade activity.

❑ Most suitable for automation, as the same tests need to be run many times.

❑ The last week of system testing should be used for regression testing of all "critical" and "high" bugs found during the system test phase.

software's functionality to evaluate if the day's build is stable enough to test. "Smoke" testing is always executed before a new release is given to the testers.

❑ The smoke test must be updated throughout the project, to keep up with the pace of software development.

❑ Smoke tests are often automated, as they are run so frequently.

❑ The TL or very senior developer typically runs the smoke test. Once passed it is their approval of the release for the users to test. Don't get a bad reputation from poor smoke testing!

The following diagram displays in which phase each of the techniques above should be applied:

Figure 12.2: Testing Techniques and when to Apply them

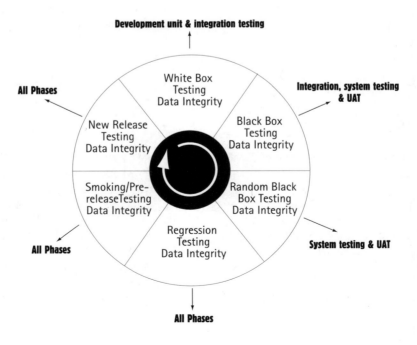

4. The Phases

Estimating Testing Time

Some rules of thumb can be applied to estimating how long your testing phase should be:

1. Life critical or safety critical systems (i.e. loss of life, health or a major environmental impact may result from undetected bugs): testing time = 50–100 per cent of development time
2. Large complex systems: testing time = 40–60 per cent of development time
3. Others: testing time = 25–50 per cent of development time.

Also don't forget the all too often *forgotten tasks*. When estimating testing time a lot of PMs forget the peripheral activities around each testing phase. Estimated peripheral activities as a low percentage allocation of development/coding duration can add as much as 120 per cent to the development time-frame for testing.

Testing Phases	% of Coding Duration
Testing preparation	15
Checkpoints/team meetings	15
Unit testing	20
Integration testing and code review	10
Documentation integration	15
System testing	25
UAT	20
Total	**120**

And that's not all! Remember the other areas:

- ✓ Training (process, tools)
- ✓ Annual leave
- ✓ Public holidays
- ✓ Sickness (allow for winter testing, colds and flus)
- ✓ Vendor delays
- ✓ User (scenario) documentation delays
- ✓ Environment set-up
- ✓ Data cleansing
- ✓ Other outside forces!

Tip:

Do not underestimate the impact of using a CAST tool (i.e. an automated test tool). If you plan on using one, build time into your estimates for training and ensure one to two team members become experts. You must really consider the benefit of using such a tool. Choosing the wrong one can sometimes can be more trouble than it's worth!

It can be hard to attain the best practice time-frames in the real world but as a PM leading a testing phase you need to start with the best practice estimates and then work backwards, depending upon budget, personnel and deadlines.

Testing Phases

Your software solution should go through the following formal testing phases:

- ✓ Unit test – see Chapter 11
- ✓ Component/module – see Chapter 11
- ✓ Integration – see Chapter 11
- ✓ System – the next phase after development:
  - – End-to-end system testing
  - – Load and stress
  - – Performance and concurrency
- ✓ UAT – the phase following system testing – the users get a chance to compare what they asked for with what they got!
- ✓ Production and rollout – follows after UAT sign-off.

The following sections briefly explain each one of these from system testing onwards to give you a basic understanding of what should be involved. For each we have provided a brief summary and associated deliverables. Where possible we have included some sample checklists. However, due to the nature of varying solutions, you will need to work very closely with the technical team to plan their implementation in detail. Remember, each phase requires detailed planning and preparation.

A Note on Building Test Cases

It is critical that good, clear, concise design specifications are available to the team and the users as these can be used to create test cases as soon as the design specifications are complete. If you can get a copy of the UAT scripts and use them in your system test phase this can really help reduce the number of bugs found in UAT!

System Test Summary

- ✓ Occurs after development is complete and signed off.
- ✓ Is usually divided into two major areas: functional and non-functional testing.
- ✓ Ensures that the execution and interaction of modules matches the intention of design specifications.
- ✓ Verifies the integrity of the full system architecture.
- ✓ Ensures that performance objectives are met.
- ✓ Ensures that code is robust and that it handles valid and invalid inputs and actions properly.
- ✓ Identifies problems with the handling of data.
- ✓ Allows the identification and fixing of bugs prior to UAT.
- ✓ Ensures that the system is stable enough for an efficient UAT phase.
- ✓ Tested by PM, QA, TL and developers, formally signed off by PM, QA lead and TL.

Warning: System testing is a critical test phase that will test the end-to-end performance functionality and usability of your system. A poor system test will mean a very bad UAT phase. From a PR point of view you really need to go into UAT with a very solid system.

Functional and Non-Functional Testing

System test is typically divided into two types of testing: functional and non-functional testing.

Functional Testing Defined

Functional testing falls into three main categories:

1. Requirements-based testing – based upon user requirements and system requirements. A tester will follow a set of defined scenarios and scripts using a variety of testing techniques
2. Business-process-based testing – for each type of user a set of tests is defined against different user profiles
3. Manual-process-based testing – don't forget the interdependencies with manual steps and procedures.

Non-Functional Testing Defined

Non-functional testing can be summarised as all the background testing, i.e. all the testing that is required to make the system reliable, stable and usable. The following areas should be tested and each will require its own plan, scripts and tools. You will need to work with various technical teams to decide areas of responsibility:

Non-Functional Testing			
❏	Memory management	❏	Compatibility
❏	Procedures	❏	Maintainability
❏	Performance and concurrency	❏	Configuration
❏	Volume	❏	Data conversion
❏	Reliability	❏	Storage
❏	Interoperability	❏	Installability
❏	Security	❏	Disaster recovery
❏	Usability	❏	Portability

As PM you need to ensure that your technical team are very focused on both the functional and the non-functional aspects while your users/testers focus on the functional side.

How Ready Are you for System Testing?

You need to define an "Are we Ready?" checklist that provides criteria that help you decide whether to begin system testing or not. System testing should not begin until development has been completed and the application meets the following criteria:

- ❏ All units of code have successfully passed unit, module and integration testing
- ❏ All "critical" and "high" bugs are fixed after the integration phase and the fixes have been regression tested
- ❏ Build and release process is stable and reliable for both the application and the database (release forward/rollback). A "smoke" test suite has been defined
- ❏ System test plan and schedule is complete
- ❏ Performance and concurrency test plan is complete
- ❏ User, performance and concurrency test scenarios are complete
- ❏ Any additional test cases for specific testing are complete
- ❏ Connectivity scenarios are complete

❏ All test scripts/drivers are complete and tested
❏ System test room/environment is set up; test machines configuration is complete
❏ The test data set is complete (accurate, sufficient volume)
❏ Test data and other supporting software are loaded (for example testing tools)
❏ Procedures for general troubleshooting are complete
❏ Testers and users are identified and trained for testing
❏ Members of IT support team are on board
❏ QA team training focusing on system testing is done and the team feels ownership of the QA/testing process.

Tip:

Often (in the real world!) some development work gets pushed back into system testing. If this happens, try to make sure it is functionality that is not on the critical path, for example reports, system administration functionality, batch scripts. You can assign an additional developer to develop and test these in parallel.

When Are you Finished System Testing?

In order to start UAT, system testing should pass the following criteria (however, these must be defined and agreed with the full team prior to system test commencement):

❏ The application meets the functional and technical requirements as stated in the design document
❏ The application satisfactorily (80 per cent) meets the performance guidelines as described in the performance and concurrency test plan.
❏ No outstanding "critical" and "high" bugs
❏ At least two successful passes through the user scenarios and test cases
❏ All operational routines have been successfully completed twice
❏ All non-functional tests are completed and signed off
❏ Team feels confident in meeting the UAT acceptance criteria as described in the UAT plan
❏ Development document is complete (i.e. updated design document)

- ❏ Operations handbook complete
- ❏ Installation guide complete.

System Test Deliverables

- ☑ Fully tested application ready for UAT.
- ☑ Updated user scenarios for UAT signed off.
- ☑ User acceptance test plan and schedule signed off.
- ☑ System test summary report including bug report of unresolved bugs by priority.
- ☑ Separate UAT test room/environment (including test data and other supporting software).
- ☑ Identified and trained testers.
- ☑ Test environment complete.
- ☑ Updated scenarios (user, performance, concurrency, connectivity – including test scripts/drivers).
- ☑ UAT environment checklist complete (data migration, directories, batch processes, user profiles).
- ☑ Updated performance and concurrency test plan.
- ☑ Updated installation guideline.
- ☑ Updated operations handbook.

Performance and Concurrency Testing

The performance of an application is a very critical part of non-functional testing and it requires detailed planning, because if application performance is not acceptable then your application is not acceptable and will not be used!

- ❏ Performance and concurrency test should commence early during the development cycle.
- ❏ True formal performance testing usually takes place in system testing and production testing. These are tests designed to track the system's performance against prescribed timings. Aim to have scripted, repeatable tests that can be timed and reproduced exactly for time comparisons.
- ❏ Concurrency testing is done by running concurrent multi-user scenarios and by random testing. These scenarios should also be run under simulated normal and peak load conditions.
- ❏ Performance testing should also be done considering the possibility of partial system failure and scalability. Remember, because most applications probably have an

impact on the overall network performance, network sizing and stress testing is of great importance.

Warning: In many cases, project teams delay performance testing until late in the development cycle, planning to "fine tune" performance problems at a later stage. This is extremely risky as in some cases performance problems may indicate a need to redesign. It is much better to start these tests as soon as code modules can be tested.

Key Areas of Focus

Performance testing should commence during development and run right through to production testing. Some of the tests will have to wait until actual production but where possible your test environment, should match the production environment, so try to complete as many tests as possible using tools or automated scripts. The following outlines high-level sample tests for performance and concurrency. It is extremely important to remember that the TL must devise a detailed structure plan for these tests.

Areas of Performance Testing

❏ Run all software applications that the user will have running simultaneously with the application.
❏ Monitor the response time for queries against the database.
❏ Monitor the impact and response times of screens running against test databases.
❏ If parts of the process fail, what is the impact on performance?
❏ Where possible use monitoring tools/utilities.
❏ Agree performance guidelines for normal conditions, peak conditions and partial system failure (benchmark figures).
❏ Build performance test scenarios.
❏ Ensure production "similar" hardware, operating system and networking software is installed and working.
❏ Run the scenarios and monitor the results.
❏ Analyse log file to see which transactions are within the time limit and outside of the time limit.
❏ Check for database query issues.
❏ Track changes as bugs are fixed.

Under Normal Conditions Test

❏ Simulate normal load.

- ❑ Check performance against production size data volume.
- ❑ Check LAN throughput verification.
- ❑ Check partial system failure.
- ❑ Scalability requirements (degradation under different loads) – data, processor speed and network bandwidth.
- ❑ Perform SQL tuning, DB query tuning, RDBMS engine tuning, LAN throughput tuning.

Stress Testing

- ❑ Carry out steps as above.
- ❑ Stress and tune the application to support peak load – identify deadlocks and application bottlenecks.
- ❑ Tune resource parameters – number and distribution of servers, size of log files, logging levels, size of temporary database space.

Network Sizing (Production)

- ❑ Network performance depends upon number of transactions per unit time and average size of a network transaction.
- ❑ Measure network traffic by:
    - Network latency – inherent delay of the network (ping to check)
    - Bandwidth usage – percentage usage of maximum available bandwidth by the application.
- ❑ Look at frequency and size of database; these will impact performance.
- ❑ Performance tuning:
    - Online vs batch
    - Database load
    - Load balancing.

Areas of Focus for Concurrency Testing

- ❑ Simulate multiple users – consider using a simulator tool.
- ❑ Test multiple users, running multiple user scenarios, accessing and modifying the same data concurrently – check for deadlocks and memory issues:
    - Multiple logins/multiple workstations
    - Multiple users simultaneously
    - Multiple users saving the same data simultaneously
    - Multiple users accessing the same data simultaneously
    - Multiple users querying the same data simultaneously.
- ❑ Test random concurrent multi-user sessions.

- ❏ Test normal load and peak load.
- ❏ With all applications running, switch back and forth between them, saving data, exiting/re-entering applications etc.
- ❏ Run all modules of the application that is being tested.
- ❏ How many screens can be open at the same time? Is there a limit?
- ❏ Add/access lots of data and perform multiple queries.
- ❏ Can you enter data at the same time in different modules?
- ❏ Is inter-module data updated correctly?
- ❏ Minimise/restore/maximise/move/close screens.
- ❏ Check memory.

The following figure summarises the various tests for performance and concurrency during system and production tests.

Figure 12.3: **Performance and Concurrency Testing in Summary**

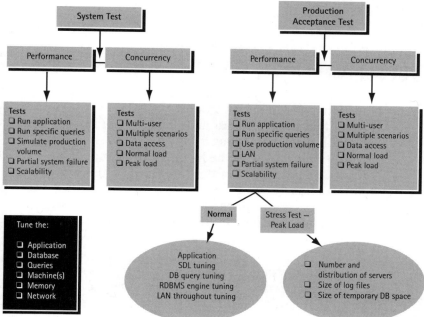

User Acceptance Testing (UAT)

UAT is the phase of a project that all development teams dread and live for at the same time. It is near the end of the project, which is good, and it is the point where you finally see if you did indeed do a good job! UAT is the hardest phase, the trickiest phase and probably the most explosive phase. It is very important to manage and structure it well. So many times we see this phase fail. UAT planning should begin at project conception. From the minute a project idea is conceived the PM must be preparing the users for this phase. You need to have buy in, resources and time commitment for the UAT phase. At the earliest stage possible you must do some PR work around UAT. You need to:

❑   Explain the need – define your user requirement, who, when, for how long, for what and where
❑   Explain the benefits – why it is in their interest to attend
❑   Explain the plan – outline your schedule
❑   Demonstrate sample UAT scenarios – prepare some sample scenarios and assign users to create the rest
❑   Define the UAT process – explain the process and how it works. Users need to be trained on how to test. Do not assume that they know how – they usually don't! UAT can be a very painful and negative experience for your users; you need to set their expectations.

UAT Summary

☑   Ensure that the application subsystems operate as per functional design specifications.
☑   Ensure that code is robust and properly handles valid and invalid inputs and actions.
☑   Identify problems with the handling of data.
☑   Identify bugs and ensure they are fixed before proceeding to production.
☑   Receive acceptance of the application from the users that it functions as defined in the design document!

Tip: Always plan to get one or two users to run their UAT test scripts towards the end of system testing. It will prepare you better for the UAT phase.

How Ready Are you for UAT?

❑ System testing has been successfully completed and signed off.
❑ The application is ready for UAT based upon the criteria agreed (all "critical" and "high" bugs are fixed and the fixes have been regression tested).
❑ Build and release process is stable and reliable for both the application and the database (release forward/rollback).
❑ UAT plan and schedule is completed and signed off.
❑ User scenarios are completed by the users, reviewed and signed off.
❑ All test scripts are complete and tested.
❑ Pre-release test suite is defined.
❑ UAT room/environment is ready. Test machines configuration is completed and verified as operational.
❑ Test environment is available for pre-release testing.
❑ Test data set is complete (accurate, sufficient volume).
❑ Test data and other supporting software are loaded (for example testing tools)
❑ Testers/users are identified and trained (i.e. testing methodology, tools demonstration and bug-fixing process).
❑ Development document update is complete.
❑ UAT kick-off presentation is complete.

UAT – Some Notes

❑ You need the best users to test the system properly.
❑ The UAT test scenarios must be extremely detailed.
❑ The UAT test scenarios form the basis of the training manual, including new procedures and processes.
❑ If you need HELP functionality get your users to create it!
❑ Try to have a separate UAT room and environment for your users.
❑ The PM is the prime contact with the users; however, always make sure at least one developer is available to the users to help with system failures, crashes, training issues etc.
❑ We recommend that the users log bugs into the bug-tracking database, but the PM and TL review them.
❑ Run daily reports for both teams – keep the users informed, start and finish each day with a status meeting.
❑ When a scenario has been tested at least twice successfully, get your users to sign it! Handing over a complete documented set of signed-off scenarios is a surer way of getting UAT approval!

When Are you Finished UAT?

UAT Acceptance Criteria

❑ The application meets the functional and technical require-ments, as stated in the design document, and any mutually agreed upon change requests.

❑ No outstanding "critical" and "high" bugs.

❑ There have been at least two successful run-throughs of every scenario.

❑ Preliminary performance acceptance agreement.

❑ Users have signed "acceptance" form.

❑ Users have created training manual.

❑ All documentation is complete.

UAT Deliverables

☑ Fully tested application ready for production testing.

☑ Documented subset of key scenarios for production testing.

☑ Documented tests that are specific to the production environment.

☑ Production environment set up, tested, reviewed and signed off.

☑ Formal handover to support team, i.e. presentation and documentation.

☑ UAT summary report including bug report of unresolved bugs/issues by priority.

☑ Production test plan and schedule signed off.

☑ User acceptance agreement.

☑ Finalised training schedule and documentation.

Production Acceptance Testing (PAT)

PAT involves the testing of the application in the production environment to ensure that the business processes (i.e. functionality) and technical requirements as stated in the design document and all mutually agreed upon change requests have been satisfied and the system is ready to be rolled out to the intended user community.

PAT Summary

☑ Ensures production environment is set up correctly, i.e. hardware, software, drivers etc.

☑ Confirms system functionality in the production environment.

☑ Ensures performance requirements have been achieved in the production environment.

☑ Ensures that start-up, shutdown, clean-up, back-up and recovery procedures work properly.

☑ Complete final documentation (with production environment nuances).

☑ Ensures user has accepted the application.

☑ Transfers ownership of the application officially to the support team and begin maintenance phase for the application.

How Ready Are you for PAT?

PAT should not begin until the application meets the following criteria:

❏ UAT is complete and the users have accepted the system functionality.

❏ The application meets the acceptance criteria described in the UAT plan (for example all "critical" and "high" bugs are fixed and the fixes have been regression tested).

❏ Build and release process is stable and reliable for both the application and the database (release forward/rollback).

❏ PAT plan and schedule is completed and signed off.

❏ Performance and concurrency tests and plans have been signed off from system testing.

❏ A subset of scenarios is defined for PAT.

❏ Operations handbook is complete with updates from system test and UAT.

❏ Installation guideline is complete with updates from system test and UAT.

❏ All technical scenarios are complete with updates from system test and UAT (for example performance, concurrency, connectivity etc.).

❏ Any additional tests that are specific to the production environment are completed.

❏ All test scripts/drivers are completed and tested.

❏ Production environment is ready (sufficient processors, memory, disk and swap space, appropriate partitioning, proper customer and server software, proper network set-up).

❏ The production data set is complete.

- Test data and other supporting software are loaded (for example testing tools).
- Users, testers and IT support are trained and ready to take ownership of the application.
- Development document update is complete.
- PAT team training is complete and the team feels ownership of the system.

When Are you Finished PAT?

The PAT process should pass the following criteria, which must be mutually agreed upon with the development and customer teams:

- The application functions correctly in the production environment and meets the functional and technical requirements as stated in the design document and all mutually agreed upon change requests.
- The application satisfactorily meets the performance guidelines as described in the performance and concurrency test plan.
- Development, code reviews, unit, module, integration, system and user acceptance testing are successfully completed.
- No outstanding "critical" and "high" bugs from the PAT phase.
- All PAT scenarios/tests have been completed.
- Production environment is working and workstations operate in accordance with design specifications.
- Support/maintenance team have taken ownership of the application.
- Executive sponsors have signed an application acceptance document.

Deliverables

- ✓ Application successfully running in the production environment.
- ✓ All user, support and operational teams are fully trained.
- ✓ Rollout procedures document handed over.
- ✓ PAT summary report including bug report of unresolved bugs by priority.
- ✓ Final documentation handed over (don't forget the issues and assumptions log!).
- ✓ Presentation of completed application to key executives, users and technical staff.

☑ Final acceptance agreement.
☑ Bug-tracking database handed over to support team.

Rollout

When the application is ready to be rolled out, you have two options: either a pilot rollout, where the application is deployed within one small group, or a full-blown rollout, where the application is rolled out across the organisation. Depending on your choice, your rollout time-frame and plan will be affected.

The objectives of the rollout phase are to ensure:

❑ The application is production-ready
❑ The users are ready go live
❑ The application goes live.

Critical Success Factors for Rollout

❑ Detailed planning with the:
  – Project team
  – Business application users
  – IT department/support team.
❑ Production testing signed off by the users.
❑ Users bought-in to using the application.
❑ Users trained in using the application.
❑ Application is production ready.
❑ Technical processes ready.
❑ Data is production ready.
❑ Business processes agreed and ready to be implemented.
❑ Rollout over a weekend/down time for the business.
❑ Back-up plan/fall-back position.
❑ Users/support own application at this point.

Rollout Activities

☑ Prepare a detailed schedule for all tasks for rollout
☑ Hold frequent checkpoints and team meetings.
☑ Prepare user's guide.
☑ Finalise development document.
☑ Generate test environment for cut-over practice.
☑ Plan for data migration.
☑ Plan for rollback.
☑ Practise installation and initial load.

✓   Carry out a dress rehearsal.
✓   Rollback if issues; otherwise celebrate!
✓   Formally hand application over to the IT department/ support team.

5. The Process

This section covers the following areas:

❑   Managing the testing process
❑   How to rate your bugs
❑   Statuses of bugs
❑   Handling enhancement/change requests
❑   A sample daily life of a bug
❑   A typical testing day
❑   Daily build and release procedures
❑   A note on test scenarios.

Managing the Testing Process

Testing requires a very structured process and an organised environment. To ensure successful testing you should be clear on the process for each day of testing. You should ensure that each day a clear schedule is outlined and each tester and developer clearly knows their tasks and responsibilities.

As a PM you should be very busy with the following:

❑   It is your duty to be fully aware what is in and what is out of scope. Testing is the most dangerous phase: when a PM does not know if a bug is genuinely a bug or if it is an enhancement, problems arise. This lack of clarity alone causes most testing phases and indeed projects to spiral out of control.
❑   Ensure the test environment is set up properly for every phase; environment problems are frustrating and are often the cause of many bugs.
❑   Agree your graduation criteria well in advance of every phase, for example "all critical and high bugs are fixed before moving to next phase".
❑   Always use a bug-tracking database or bug-tracking forms. Remember, the bug-tracking database will become your help

file for the support team – insist on a very high standard of how developers document their fixes.

❑ Ensure all test scenarios are tested at least twice before sign-off.

❑ Ensure your users are trained upfront on the testing and fixing process.

❑ Run daily status reports indicating how many bugs are outstanding, their status and any updates.

❑ You should be very clear about your bug severity definitions (see below) and the team must recognise that you and the TL "own" the bug ratings. Any disagreement around them can be resolved in the weekly status meetings.

❑ No developer should estimate or fix an enhancement/change request without agreement and consent from the PM.

How to Rate your Bugs

The following is a sample set of bug ratings; you must agree the ratings with your team and customer.

Sample Bug Severity Ratings

❑ Critical – system not functioning, a crash, data loss, inability to access functionality.

❑ High – functionality is significantly impaired, task cannot be completed; a major workaround is necessary.

❑ Medium – functionality is somewhat impaired; a minor workaround is necessary.

❑ Low – functionality can be accomplished; either an annoyance is present or efficiency can be improved.

❑ Cosmetic – a minor modification to the appearance of the interface to improve usability, for example colours, labels

❑ Enhancement/change request – a change from the original design specification is required.

Tip: Sometimes it is a good idea not to allow the medium rating! It forces clearer division between high and low bugs.

Statuses of Bugs

The following is a sample set of statuses that bugs can have; you should tailor these for your project.

Sample Status of Bugs

❑ **Open** – a bug is found.
❑ **Issue** – the bug needs further research and is put onto the issue log.
❑ **Enhancement** – the bug relates to functionality that is not defined in this phase of the application.
❑ **Assigned** – the bug is assigned to a developer to be fixed and is currently in progress.
❑ **Not a bug** – the bug is not a true bug; it is a tester misunderstanding.
❑ **Cannot reproduce** – the developer cannot reproduce the bug.
❑ **Fixed** – the bug has been resolved by the developer and is ready to be tested.
❑ **Duplicate** – the bug is a duplicate of another bug. (In this case, the duplicate ID should be noted. It is possible that fixing one does not correct the other, in which case they were not duplicates of the same problem and the one still failing should be re-classified as open.)
❑ **Tested/closed** – the bug has been tested and passed the test twice! This means the bug is now closed.
❑ **Tested, not fixed** – the bug has been tested but does not pass the test.
❑ **Signed off** – the bug has been tested and approved by the users/testers.
❑ **Enhancement/change request** – the bug is not a bug but a change request or an enhancement to the original design specification.

Handling Enhancement/Change Requests

When an enhancement/change request comes in always refer back to your design document and requirements matrix for a detailed assessment of the request. For every enhancement you should get your TL and developers to formally estimate and document the work involved (technical complexity), using your design specifications, and get your users to rate it based upon business benefit and organisational readiness. Between the two teams you can then decide how critical the enhancement actually is.

You should expect change requests; there may have been outside changes that need to be accommodated within the project but they must be assessed on all levels, i.e. their impact on:

❑ Business process
❑ Technical design
❑ Project delivery date
❑ Budget.

Always document your findings for each request and make the executive sponsor aware if the request will affect project delivery date or budget.

 Warning: Badly estimated enhancements and change requests combined with a weak PM can throw a project into turmoil!

(See Appendix 12.1 for sample enhancement/change request form.)

Sample Daily Life of a Bug

Figure 12.4 represents the typical daily flow of a bug. It should be presented to all users at the start of UAT.

Figure 12.4: Sample Daily Life of a Bug

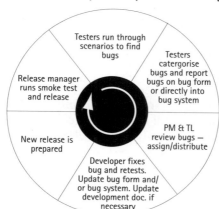

Some Points to Note

Testers run through their test scenarios to find bugs. Make sure any complicated error messages that appear on screen are captured. These sometimes can be quite complicated so the easiest way to do this is to get the tester to hit the "Print Screen" button on the keyboard, paste the image into a word processing document and attach it to a bug form for submission. (See Appendix 12.2 for sample bug report form.)

Testers categorise bugs and report bugs on bug form or directly into bug system. If you have very good testers who are used to testing you may decide to let them enter their bugs directly into the bug system. However, for more novice testers we suggest that they document their bugs on paper bug forms.

PM and TL review bugs, assign and distribute. The PM and TL review the bug reports and possibly reassign their ratings in case there are rating discrepancies with the users – you don't want a developer working on a "high" bug when it is in fact an "enhancement"! Remember, often a bug is not a bug at all – just a training issue. As PM you must watch these; if they constantly arise you may have a usability issue.

Developer fixes bug and retests. Update development document. When a developer fixes a bug they must enter in the bug system exactly how they fixed that problem. At the end of the testing phase you can then hand over the bug system to the support team. If a fundamental change has been made to resolve the bug the developer must also update the development document. Remember, when a user scenario has been passed make sure your tester signs the passed scenario document. It supports the user acceptance.

A new release is prepared. Developers must focus daily on fixing all high and critical bugs. Once the TL is satisfied that all these bugs are fixed and documented a new release can be created. Don't forget the back-up procedures and check-in and check-out procedures!

Release manager runs smoke test and release. Make sure the release is tested successfully at least twice before re-releasing for the next day's testing. Ensure the test environment and data are clean. Start each day with clean data, a new release and a status report for your users.

A Typical Testing Day

❑ Start each morning with a joint team meeting – daily goals, scenarios to be tested, questions etc.

❑ Users/testers should test Monday to Thursday.

❑ Fridays should be kept free to allow time to:
  – Run status and review meetings with management teams and users
  – Review outstanding bugs, issues
  – Negotiate enhancements
  – General clean-up duties, documentation.

❑ Ensure one hour each day is allocated for random black box testing.

❑ Build a new release every night to start "clean" every morning.

Sample Schedule

Day	Users/Testers Schedule	Development/QA Team Schedule
Tuesday	9:00–9:30 Joint kick-off meeting	9:00–9:30 Joint kick-off meeting
	10:00–12:00 Scenario testing	10:00–12:00 Bug fixing/ documentation/user support
	12:00–1:00 LUNCH	12:00–1:00 LUNCH
	1:00–3:00 Scenario testing	1:00–4:00 Bug fixing/ documentation/user support
	3:00–4:00 Random black-box testing	4:00–6:00 Bug fixing/clean up
	4:00–4:30 Wrap-up meeting	6:00–6:30(!) Status meeting/daily Build/Release

Daily Build and Release Procedures

It is critical that your entire team understand and implement the build and release procedures. Managing the application code can be difficult unless the procedures have been defined clearly. We recommend the following:

❑ All developers should merge code changes into a private copy of the master source files

❑ Delivery team should build and test a private release before smoke testing

❑ Delivery team should execute the smoke test to ensure code is working

❏ Delivery team should check the new code into the master source files. This should be coordinated through the TL/release manager and should only be carried out at specific agreed times – aim for same time every day
❏ TL/release manager should generate and approve the daily build
❏ Always run the smoke test twice to ensure stability
❏ Fix any problems immediately and re-test!

A Note on Test Scenarios

Application testing is based upon a number of components including test cases and user scenarios. Test cases describe steps/actions to be taken for testing the application and the expected results. User scenarios describe these steps/actions and expected results from "a day in the life of a user" perspective. Typically, user scenarios describe (a part of) the business process that the application supports. Both test cases and user scenarios are used to test and demonstrate the correct operation of the application in meeting the requirements that are outlined in the design document. The following provides hints for designing test cases and user scenarios:

❏ Test case independence – a test case should not depend on the success of the previous one in order to run
❏ Start and end points – define where the test case starts and ends in the application; also define how to navigate to the place where the test case needs to run
❏ No gap, no overlap – test cases must cover all important business functions, avoiding excessive clustering around major functions and gaps around other functions
❏ Keep it simple – do not make test cases overly complex; break them down as much as possible.

Experiences from previous projects show that one user scenario might take a user two to five hours to write and verify. We recommend the following:

❏ Each window must be included in at least one scenario, ideally two
❏ Each major piece of functionality from the requirements matrix must be included in at least one scenario
❏ Write shorter scenarios as opposed to a few long scenarios

❏ Focus on the business reasoning behind the scenario
❏ Provide enough detail to demonstrate how to execute the scenario without getting too caught up in buttons being pushed and fields being enabled and disabled.

Users have the responsibility for developing robust and detailed user scenarios since they have the most in-depth, first-hand understanding of the real-life business situations the applications must support and understand the special needs of the user community. As PM you should, however, support this effort and ensure that the user scenarios are completed before system testing begins.

6. The Testing Tools

Automated testing is a very valuable asset to the testing phase of any project. Implemented correctly with the proper environment and support structures it can help ensure a very smooth and thorough testing phase.

At the time of the writing of this book, we counted at least 292 different types of reputable CAST tools on the market. In general they can range from GUI to performance to dynamic analysis tools.

However, don't jump in too quickly in using a CAST tool; there is a lot of upfront work required before you can even think about using one. You need to assess your environment and team readiness before investing in one, or indeed many. If you are thinking about automated testing, the following points should be noted:

✓ Automated testing must be automating a formalised manual testing process that is already in use. You need to create this first.
✓ Decide what to automate. Analyse your applications, procedures and processes to determine which are suited to automation before evaluating a CAST tool.
✓ Detailed test cases are required, including predictable "expected results", which have been developed from design specifications. Be focused on scripts; they must be reusable, repeatable and maintainable.
✓ A stand-alone test environment is required, including a test database that is restorable to a known constant, so that the test cases are able to be repeated each time there are modifications made to the application.
✓ There is often a personnel impact when a dedicated CAST

● ●

tool support role(s) is required. Allow time for training.

✓ Go for the quick wins – the best use and purpose of automated test tools is to automate regression testing, so it is a good idea to start here.

✓ To be successful you must develop a database of detailed test cases that are repeatable; this suite of tests should be run every time there is a change to the application to ensure that the change does not produce unintended consequences.

✓ Automation will not replace the human factor necessary to test an application – be realistic about what can actually be tested.

✓ Choose an appropriate tool for the type of application you are working with.

✓ Don't pick one without using a definitive selection methodology – use a formal package selection methodology with scorecard results.

✓ Look at your environment – there is no tool on the market that can be used to support all environments; you should plan well into the future.

✓ Always test the vendor – get references and demonstrations bespoke for your environment and application.

✓ Always start with a pilot project of the implementation.

✓ Agree processes and standards across the organisation. Publish scripting standards and work to make the tool fit your current testing process.

It Could Happen to you ...

Bossy Consultants

As a relatively new PM on one of my first external projects for a customer I was faced with a situation that nowadays I'd slap on the head with one strike no questions asked! We were developing a new application that required radical new business processes for the customer moving them from a paper to paperless environment. There were three teams on the project, i.e. my delivery team, the customer team and a very high-profiled business consultancy team who managed the definition and implementation of the customer's new business processes.

We had gone through a pretty successful four-month development phase with many model office shows. Consensus was high and there was generally an air of excitement moving into the testing phase. However, while setting up for system test the external business consultants decided that they and the customer team should start the UAT phase. To us, this was nuts! Why start users testing something that hasn't even been through rigorous system testing? I disagreed vehemently giving all the relevant reasons. My biggest worry was two-fold: the bad PR the application would get and the distraction to my delivery team. My lack of experience and confidence maybe made me lose the fight that ensued. I gave in on the condition that they would not distract us and we would not support their unstable environment. How naïve! I would never again lose that fight.

When the users got their unstable environment they started logging bugs – of course! The TL was demented by constant calls to solve crashes; the users weren't formally prepared for UAT; word was getting out that the delivery team did not do a good job. The atmosphere was dreadful – both teams ended up despising each other! Eventually through tears and distress on the users' side they agreed to wait for formal UAT. We were saved! But the delivery team had been put through unnecessary anguish during what is a stressful phase anyway.

To this day that customer has praised the application and is always a willing reference site; and to this day I have never budged on sticking to a strict testing regime, i.e. the one we have outlined to you above!

Appendix 12.1: Sample Enhancement/Change Request Form

Submitted by:		Request No.:	«NUMBER»
Module:		Date:	
Design Doc. Page No.(s):		Time:	
Screen/Function Involved:		Closed: Y/N	

Change Description		Required		Desired		Nice	

Development Team Only

Reviewed by:	
Module Name:	
Item Name:	
Effort Assessment (days/hours):	
Solution Strategy	T (Trade),
	ICX (Increase Scope at Customer Expense)
	DTO (Delivery Team Oversight)
	E (Next Phase Enhancement)
	W (Manual Work Around)

Type		Impact		Priority	
Bug Fix		Screen		Critical	
Cosmetic		Database		High	
Enhancement		Function		Low	
		API Function		Future	

Resolution

Resolved by:	<Delivery team person>
Actual Effort to Resolve (days):	
User Sign-off Date:	

Resolution Description

<How it all worked out>

Appendix 12.2: Sample Bug Report Form

Window Name/Function:
Environment: **Internal Problem No.:**
Submitter's Name: **SW Version:**
Assigned To: **Duplicate of No.:**
Date:

Priority: Critical High *Medium* Low Enhancement (circle one)

Short Description   (1 line description,)

[ ]

Detailed Issue Description (more details — as much information as possible, for example what were you doing etc.)

[ ]

Error message (attach a print screen of error, if possible; if not detail exactly the error that appeared on the screen)

[ ]

For Development Use Only
Fixed By: **Fixed Date:**
Window/Function Fixed: **SW Version:**
Time Spent in Hours:

Problem Type: (circle one)
Interface   Functionality   Database   Connectivity

Resolution Description

[ ]

Developer Notes

[ ]

Test Notes

[ ]

CHAPTER 13

Project Planning and Estimation

"A project will be estimated differently by team members depending upon key factors such as day, the time and the wind chill factor!"

Project Planning in a Nutshell

To deliver a project successfully, you must create appropriate project plans to guide you and your team from the beginning to the end of your project. Each plan describes all of the tasks, time-frames, milestones and resources needed to deliver the project or project phase. The PM monitors the project plan(s) constantly to see whether the team is on time, behind or maybe even ahead of schedule. Project plans need to be as detailed as possible as soon as possible.

Estimation in a Nutshell

Estimation is the process of "judging" the effort, cost and time-frames for a project, by using what you know you have to deliver, the background from the customer, your team's previous experience, your team's "know-how" and some rules of thumb.

Project Planning

There are many project plans that you may have to create during a project lifecycle. These may include the following:

- ✓ Quality plan
- ✓ Development plan
- ✓ Activity/task plan

- ✓ Milestone plan
- ✓ People plan
- ✓ Budgetary plan
- ✓ Test and integration plan
- ✓ Release plan
- ✓ Operations and support plan
- ✓ Training plan
- ✓ Model office plan
- ✓ Change and organisation plan
- ✓ Wrap-up plan.

Many of the above may be merged into a single plan – it is up to you how you actually create your plans. The important thing is that your plan covers all aspects of your project delivery, that you have detailed your tasks at a sufficient level and that you have assigned responsibility for each task of every plan.

There are a number of project management tools out there to help you manage these plans. We recommend Mircosoft Office Enterprise Project Management Solution. However, these are only tools that facilitate creating and managing the project plan – your project plan could just be on a sheet of paper or in a spreadsheet – what is key is that you have all the activities identified, all timelines defined and all resources assigned and that the plan is kept current.

Being able to use a project management tool doesn't mean you know how to define project plans. A plan goes wrong when a PM, through inexperience, omits tasks from a project plan.

Some Common Terms in Project Planning

The following are common project management terms. You may not use all of them but it is good to be aware of them.

Milestone

An identifiable key event/target and a great excuse to get paid! Your milestones should be typically every four to six weeks and are generally associated with key deliverables, for example release of an application component into a model office.

Schedule (GANTT Chart)
Distribution of work or deliverables over time, i.e. a list of tasks along a timeline.

Network Diagram (PERT Chart)
A logical structured way of linking dependencies between areas, or Work Breakdown Structure (WBS).

Work Breakdown Structure (WBS)
A logical, structured way of defining and dividing larger components of work, for example:

Help desk – functionality (component)
- ❑ Design new procedures
- ❑ Install technology
- ❑ Recruit staff
- ❑ Test new procedures
- ❑ Test technology
- ❑ Train staff.

Task
The smallest unit of work that can be tracked and estimated. The following are associated with each task:

- ❑ Skills required
- ❑ Man hours required, i.e. the number of people x duration x eight hours (working day)
- ❑ Resources required
- ❑ Elapsed time – duration end to end (if you assume only one person working on it).

Critical Path
The minimum duration of your project. It is based upon activities that must occur sequentially. Tasks that are part of the critical path cannot be delayed without the end date of the project being delayed too.

Project Plan Must Dos

Each plan contains a list of tasks along a timeline with resources assigned to each task and a set of milestones that will lead to completion of your project. For each plan you should:

- ✓ List all tasks in the plan at their lowest level – you can do summary views when required, but you need to identify all tasks that need to be completed
- ✓ Create milestones and checkpoints throughout the plan to continually assess the project and get feedback and reviews
- ✓ Know your critical path, i.e. the minimum critical set of tasks that must be followed in order to deliver the core functionality of the solution
- ✓ Assume time in your project plan for your team being unavailable, i.e. vacation, sickness, training
- ✓ Keep your project plan(s) up to date – update at least weekly. This is your barometer for how the project is progressing. If this is out of date, then there is a good chance your project is too
- ✓ Identify the resources needed for the tasks and if they are not available, assign training time for the resources that are.
- ✓ Monitor your workload balancing
- ✓ Keep your team updated on their weekly tasks through the weekly team meetings – listing all of their tasks for the week ahead
- ✓ Remember, if you put multiple resources against a task/component, ensure it can be sub-divided up across the resources
- ✓ Keep your customer updated on their weekly tasks through the weekly customer meetings – listing all of their tasks for the week ahead too!

Two fundamental project plans that must always be created for an IT project are the design project plan and the development project plan. The following outlines sample tasks to ensure you have important topics covered in these critical plans:

Design Project Plan	Development Project Plan
Preparation Organise project staffing Review/submit technical questionnaire Finalise design plan and detail schedule Environment set-up Review client documentation Training Arrange logistics (meeting rooms, supplies, access to client's site etc.) Kick-off (delivery and customer team) – including norming **System Interfaces Design** External list Internal list **Screen Design** Define GUI standards Screen flow Menu design Application components and associated windows **Function Design** Design standard functions (e.g. close window) Design specific functions – list each major functional area **Reports Design** Report 1, 2, 3 ... – list and define all reports **Logical Database Design** High-level sizing exercise Design transaction tables Design reporting tables Build ERD diagram Design stored procedures or SQL as required **Software Architecture** **Processes** Design processes framework Design upload, download processes etc. **User Interface** Application framework Error handling Message handling Other **Hardware Architecture** Define sizing requirements Select hardware Design security Identify software requirements Identify performance requirements Network requirements **Data Migration** Data area to be migrated – from what date? **System Administration** Design back-up/archive processes Design audit trail Design user maintenance – role based? Archiving Disaster recovery **Other** Issues and risk management **Overall Project Management** Development planning Team management Document production – standards, chapter owners etc. Document review QA reviews Team meetings Customer meetings Checkpoints and milestones Workshops Final customer presentation Public holidays	**Preparation** Organise project staffing Technical review Finalise development plan and detail schedule Set-up environment Review client documentation Training Arrange logistics (meeting rooms, supplies, access to client's site etc.) Kick-off (delivery and customer team) – including norming Set up coding standards (user interface, SQL, unix, C or C++ etc.) **Environment Set-up** Hardware installation Database install Database build User interface install Source control install Other library install Configure makefile Build common functions and/or classes **Interfaces Development** External – list Internal – list **Screen Development** Build generic functions or classes (e.g. error handling) Build generic data access functions or classes Build common user interface functionality (look-ups, calculation, validation etc.) Build login windows Build menu subsystem Build specific windows – list all **Review** Code reviews Bug fixing **Function Development** Develop standard functions (e.g. close window) Develop specific functions – list all **Review** Code review Bug fixing **Reports Development** Build report templates Build reports – list all **Database development** Build database Build transaction tables Build reporting tables Modify ERD diagram (as required) Develop stored procedures or SQL as required **Software Architecture** **Processes** Ensure availability of third-party machines Create scripts (if applicable) Build interface applications **User Interface** Application framework Error handling Message handling Other **Hardware Architecture** Install hardware Develop security Install software Test performance **Data Migration** Build scripts to load appropriate data Load appropriate data

Public holidays
Vacation
Sickness

Load appropriate data
System Administration
    Build back-up scripts
    Build security
    Develop user maintenance — role based?
Other
    Issue and risk assessment
Project Management
    Ongoing development planning
    Team management
    Document production
    QA reviews
    Team meetings
    Customer meetings
    Checkpoints
    Workshops
    Customer presentation
    Public holidays
    Vacation
    Sickness

Estimation

One of the key points of failure when delivering projects is the estimation process. When you commit to delivering a project, you must be happy that you have estimated all aspects of the project and that you have allocated enough time for each. You can read books upon books on the estimation process for IT solutions but often the mistake is not with the mathematical calculation, it is with the estimation process, i.e. when estimates were done and who was involved.

When estimating, it is important to:

- ☑ Schedule time with the full delivery team to prepare, estimate and review the final estimates
- ☑ Leverage knowledge from outside your team, for example other teams, technical experts, research etc.
- ☑ Record all constraints, risks, issues identified with every estimate
- ☑ Document all assumptions and customer's expectations with every estimate.

Warning: There is a simple rule of thumb when estimating that PMs under pressure will often forget: try to never give a definite implementation estimate until the design phase is completed. You can give a low to high range but never commit to a definitive time-frame or cost. PMs can find this hard to enforce. However, if, for example, you are building a house you will not get completed costs for the finished structure until you present your architects plans! We all accept this, don't we?

You should have two key estimation exercises during the lifecycle of an IT project:

1. Estimating design (after scope of course!) – producing definite design phase time-frames and costs and a low to high range for implementation based upon agreed phasing, assumptions, roles, responsibilities, team size and technologies
2. Estimating implementation (after design of course!) – producing definite development, testing and rollout time-frames and costs based upon agreed phasing, assumptions, roles, responsibilities, team size and technologies.

Estimating Design

Your estimate for design duration should be based upon what you have found out during the scope phase and all the information you have about the project to date and any previous projects that were similar. The areas you need to think about are:

Estimate Area	Tasks
Preparation	❑ Review scope deliverable (processes, requirements, business case etc.) ❑ Review issues and risks log and any constraints that may exist ❑ Team set-up, norming etc. ❑ Environment set-up ❑ Training ❑ Logistics ❑ External vendor interaction (if applicable) **Estimate depends upon the size of the project and commitment of customer team. Ranges from 2 days to 2 weeks.**
Business processes and business case	❑ Review and refine business processes ❑ Review and refine business case **Rule of thumb estimates are as follows for business processes – allow:**

	❑ High process complexity: 2–3 days ❑ Medium process complexity: 1 day ❑ Low process complexity: 1/2 day ❑ Simple process complexity: 2 hours
User design, i.e. screens, screen flow, look and feel	Based upon the requirements matrix estimate the complexity of each group/module of requirements. Complexity is based upon: ❑ How much is known and not known about the module ❑ How complex the process is ❑ How many screens will be required ❑ How complex the requirement is ❑ Do you feel the "To Be" business processes are signed off or will there be a lot of changes? You will need to estimate for potential changes if sign-off has not been achieved before design. Estimate time for review of the designed screens, looking at screens and screen flow, overall look and feel and business rules. **Rule-of-thumb estimates for user interface design are as follows:** ❑ High complexity: 3–4 days ❑ Medium complexity: 2–3 days ❑ Low complexity: 1 day
Functional components	Complex functionality, such as complex calculation engines, needs to be estimated separately and workshops will be needed to gather all the rules etc. **Estimates for these depend on the complexity of the functionality you are trying to design. See Chapter 10 for function specifications.**

Technical design	You need to ensure you estimate time for the design of the following sample topics. Add time for technical QA too.
	<table><tr><td>Conceptual architecture</td><td>Hardware architecture</td></tr><tr><td>Software architecture</td><td>Database</td></tr><tr><td>Network</td><td>Reporting</td></tr><tr><td>Connectivity (internal and external)</td><td>Error handling</td></tr><tr><td>Internationalisation</td><td>Performance and concurrency</td></tr><tr><td>Operational procedures (batch jobs etc.)</td><td>System administration</td></tr><tr><td>Security</td><td>Manuals, guides etc.</td></tr><tr><td>Online help</td><td></td></tr></table>
Documentation	**Depending upon the size of the project this could range from 3 days to 2 weeks. Typically documentation time is 10–15% of the total time allocated to a phase.** Allow time for: ❑ Document template set-up ❑ Document creation ❑ Document collation ❑ Document review (internally by team) ❑ Document review (externally by QA person) ❑ Printing
Other/Peripheral	**Don't forget the peripheral tasks:** ❑ Project planning for next phases – development, testing, rollout and support ❑ Meetings and checkpoints ❑ Public holidays and vacation ❑ Sickness (especially if winter project!)

The "Other/Peripheral" tasks are always underestimated and potentially most crucial. Here is an example of how a six-week design phase (thirty days) can be impacted by these. Holidays, vacation and sickness are not included! Twenty-one days are omitted in total.

Fixed Phase	Design %	6 Week
Design preparation	15	4.5
Checkpoints	10	3
Team meetings	10	3
QA	10	3
Documentation integration & wrap-up	20	6
Next phase estimates	5	1.5
Total	**70**	**21**

A Note on Estimating Implementation before Design is Complete

If you are estimating beyond the design phase (before design) you will have to base your low and high-level estimates upon the components identified in the requirements matrix. You will have to produce an informed "guesstimate" rather than an estimate. You will need to assess the following:

- ✓ Estimated business process impact
- ✓ Estimated number of windows and menu
- ✓ Estimated number of functions
- ✓ Estimated number of reports
- ✓ Estimated complexity of data
- ✓ Estimated complexity of data migration
- ✓ Estimated points of integration
- ✓ Estimated complexity of architecture (not necessarily known yet)
- ✓ Estimated complexity of software solution (not necessarily known yet)
- ✓ Estimated training implications
- ✓ Estimated testing complexity
- ✓ Estimated complexity of rollout
- ✓ Estimated complexity of user administration
- ✓ Estimated complexity of system administration
- ✓ Estimated team size and skill set available
- ✓ Current issues, risks and assumptions
- ✓ Customer's IT strategy
- ✓ Documentation that will be required.

You should make it very clear to your customer that you have produced a "guesstimate" and that there are many unknowns, which you will have listed of course! These unknowns can only be clarified after the design phase has been completed.

Tip: We have worked on different projects where the design phase ranged from two weeks to sixteen weeks. Try not to let the design phase be less than one week to allow for detailed documentation and wrap up. Also monitor carefully your phasing exercise if a design phase is estimated at over sixteen weeks.

Estimating Implementation (i.e. Development, Testing and Rollout)

After the design phase, you will have detailed specifications for all windows, reports, functions, connectivity, databases etc. You will know the hardware and software architecture and be able to assess resource requirements and the level of training that may be required.

The process for estimating implementation at this point is as follows:

Estimation Process
Pre-requisite – team review the design document.
Gather the entire team in a room.
Review all issues, risks and assumptions.
Agree development estimates for high, medium and low complexity for windows, functions, reports etc.
Estimate all windows, reports, functions required. For each, estimate time for: ❑   Coding ❑   Documentation of code and updating of the development document ❑   Unit testing ❑   Performance testing.
Estimate technical areas: ❑   System administration ❑   User administration ❑   Security ❑   Integration with internal and external systems ❑   Data migration and upload ❑   Error handling ❑   Back-up and recovery ❑   Disaster recovery ❑   Documentation.

Estimate testing time based upon coding time
Remember:
- ❏ Component testing
- ❏ Integration testing
- ❏ System testing
- ❏ Performance testing
- ❏ User acceptance testing
- ❏ Pre-production testing.

Estimate other tasks (Sample percentages of coding duration):
- ❏ Preparation: 15%
- ❏ Code reviews: 10%
- ❏ Document review and production: 20%
- ❏ Checkpoints: 10%–15%
- ❏ Model office (if applicable): 10%
- ❏ Weekly status meetings with team and customer
- ❏ Public holidays
- ❏ Vacation
- ❏ Training
- ❏ Sickness (allow for a winter project!).

Estimate resource needs – full-time and part-time.

Determine contingency – you may need to add up to 20% of overall project time depending upon the risks and issues outstanding. Some rules of thumb:
- Scope: 5% contingency
- Design: 10% contingency
- Development: 15–20% contingency.

Estimate cost, based on time and resources needed.

Build project plan.

It Could Happen to you ...

Everyday Estimation Errors!

During the estimation process of a project, there was as assumption made by a customer that was thankfully documented in the design document, i.e. "The Cobol routines in the legacy system are callable". Seem like an innocuous statement? As a result of this, the development estimate was based upon the developers simply having to "call" these routines and get the data they needed back. Upon reaching development, however, it turned out that this was not the case – the Cobol routines were *not* callable! The development time-frame grew significantly and code needed to be written to get the data. The team was fortunately covered in negotiating with the customer for a viable workaround (other functionality was dropped!) as the customer had read and signed off the design document. The delivery team was saved!

All assumptions should be challenged during an estimation session and even tested to ensure that they are correct; at least if you have it documented there is room for negotiation!

Web Projects

"On the web, a fortune is spent on technology but don't forget technology doesn't do the buying!"

The Web Project in a Nutshell

All IT projects can follow the same project methodology we have outlined in this book. However, an IT project that has a web/ebusiness/internet/intranet implication requires some additional analysis, which needs to be considered when completing the scope, design, development and testing phases. The following need to be considered and analysed for all web projects:

❑ Target audience
❑ Content architecture
❑ Visual architecture
❑ Additional role requirements
❑ Web testing.

The risk of web projects takes on a whole new dimension. Common areas of concern are: browser configuration, performance scalability, reliability and above all security.

Target Audience

Your target audience is the group(s) and type of people you would expect to use your website. You need to identify who is your target market. The following is a sample of what needs to be considered when assessing the target audience implications of a website:

✓ User description – the user community
✓ Target user – age, gender, geographical location, language etc.
✓ The browser to suit all users
✓ Minimum bandwidth the website will be used with. Remember to consider number and size of images of content and the overall supporting content and visual architectures
✓ Competitive analysis – understand your competitors and assess their website's good features
✓ Required features – identification of key features that you would want, but also elimination of features that would not work
✓ Unique proposition from this website – definition of the key points that would draw people to the website and keep them there.

Content Architecture

The content architecture should start at the scope phase. It identifies the information that is to be published on the site. A content spreadsheet should be set-up and maintained which will be used in conjunction with your requirements matrix. The content spreadsheet and site map, along with the target audience definition, will help identify the cognitive and visual architectures (look-and-feel) and overall organisation of the website. Content architecture also identifies the data to be stored and managed for the site. It will identify the data manipulation/transformation needs and content that will need to be created dynamically. The content spreadsheet should include headings such as:

Content Spreadsheet	Description
Subject area	Information area
Information definition	Individual content within an area
Information source and transfer mechanism	Where will the data come from and how will it be transferred to the website?
Information format	In what format is the data?
Target user groups	Describe user groups for data
Update frequency	How often will the data be updated?

Warning: Do not underestimate the time required to gather content for a website. It is always hugely underestimated! The dependency upon users, suppliers, partners, business units etc. is a major risk in itself. Depending upon volumes, you may want to think about a dedicated content manager role and/or automated content management tool.

Visual Architecture

The visual architecture defines the look and feel of pages within a website. It contains all of the page layouts, page organisation and flow and associated creative details. You need to define an underlying standard look and feel that is the basis for the design of all pages on the site. To define the visual architecture you need to do the following types of activities:

❑ **Assess your competitors** – review competitor or other websites to assess the quality and effectiveness of the creative aspects of their websites. Look at areas such as the following:
  - Strengths and weaknesses
  - Branding
  - Page layout
  - Navigation design
  - Look and feel
  - Colour scheme
  - Animation
  - Overall consistency
  - Content hierarchy
  - Advertising.

❑ **Review your brand** – branding is your identity and your audience should remember you by it. Branding is critical. If people like your brand and your site, they will keep coming back and will tell other people to use it!

❑ **Build the navigation map** – it is defined by page layout, webpage elements and site structure. It is how the user will navigate through the site. This includes an understanding of where they are, where they can go and where they have been. Remember, there are two key areas to define:
  1. The global map – items that remain in the same location on every page within the site

2. The local map – items that change location depending upon where you are in the site.

❑ **Unique creative elements** – the set of unique creative elements to be used to support the corporate brand and design goals of the site, for example colours, fonts, images etc. You will need to mock-up a few options!

❑ **The style sheet** – establishes the guidelines and standards that provide basic layout and mandatory features for the webpages, for example font typeface and style, colour, image pixel sizes etc.

Tip: You will need to review your technical architecture options to support your web project. For this type of project, areas like security, bandwidth, user load and scalability will be of particular importance.

Additional Role Requirements

There are a number of additional roles that you need to consider when doing a web implementation:

❑ Visual designer – designs the information flow and the "feel" of the site for the user

❑ Creative specialist – website creative look

❑ Web developers – latest web programming skills, for example XML, OO etc.

❑ Marketing expert – branding, target audience definition etc.

❑ Technical expert – ensure your TL has the security knowledge and expertise.

❑ Content manager – managing content flow, different formats, data etc.

❑ Website manager – responsible for maintenance and monitoring of website

❑ Hosting company – some companies provide hosting facilities for a website after it has been rolled out – these will need to be considered early on in the project and added to the project costs.

Warning: When building a website for your customer, one of the biggest issues that must be pointed out to them is order fulfilment. If you build a site to sell products, the underlying processes within your customer's organisation must be able to support the demand for products that the website may generate. If it does not the site is doomed to failure. If you are let down by a website, you never have to visit it again!

Web Testing

In addition to everything outlined in Chapter 12, as a project manager of a web project you should be extremely focused upon reliability, scalability, performance and above all security for the application. The following outlines some of the extra areas of focus required for a web project, especially during the testing phase:

❑ Web-specific tests:
  - Static testing, for example HTML, browser syntax, visuals
  - Link checking
  - Object loads and performance
  - Transaction verification
  - Reliability
  - Availability and usability
  - Security
  - Shopping cost price, tax and shipping calculations
  - Database, file, table validation, data integrity
  - Multiple browser compatibility
  - Payment transaction security
  - Style guides/sheets
  - Pop-ups
  - Middleware testing
  - Screen size and pixel resolution
  - Cookies
  - Load time
  - Site navigation and hyperlinks
  - Correct data capture
  - Gateway software
  - Server load testing
  - Response times (guides, pages etc.)
  - Printer friendly pages

- – Client versus server validation and functional positioning
- – Site map
- – Audio/video streaming content
- – Searchable documents
- – Frames
- – Information architecture
- ❏ Tools for web testing, for example:
  - – Browser test tools
  - – Security checking and auditing
  - – External site monitors
  - – HTML validators
  - – Performance test tools
  - – Security checking and auditing
- ❏ Points of integration
  - – External and legacy systems
- ❏ Content management
- ❏ Interactive customer management.

It Could Happen to you ...

The Website that Waffled!

We were once asked to do a customer assessment on a website that was implemented for a large car dealership. It was a cool new site with the best of features and glowed about customer service, customer loyalty and customer rewards etc. So we decided to do a simple test.

Through the "Contact Us" link on the site we submitted an order for a new car. We outlined the car type, the colour, engine size and any additional features that would bump up the price! Our test was to see how long it would take the dealership to contact us and process our order. To our amazement, the dealership never contacted us at all. A lovely, expensive website that just waffled!

CHAPTER 15

Project Wrap-Up

"Always take time to review – harvest what went well and learn from what went wrong."

Wrapping-up your Project in a Nutshell

Sometimes it is very hard for a team to know when a project is actually over. Very often in the IT world project teams are reallocated to other projects, sometimes in the later stages of UAT or even during production testing. Some team members get lost in support roles developing scoped out enhancements or changing cosmetic requests. Of course, depending upon the project success there can be a fanfare of farewells, cake and congratulations all round or else a silent whisper of failed embarrassment! What rarely happens is a formal project closure phase. This is time that is really required whether a project has been a success or not. Project wrap-up time of at least five days should be added to every project plan. There are key components to wrapping up projects that are often neglected:

❑ Project reviews
❑ Sunset reviews
❑ Project harvesting
❑ Case studies
❑ Benefit analysis.

Project Reviews

At the end of a project always remember to thank your delivery team and indeed anyone who helped you throughout the project.

Believe it or not, this rarely happens! It is up to you as PM to ensure that the management team understand how hard your team worked to deliver the project. Besides receiving a formal "thank you" the most important thing you can give a team member is a formal review that will feed into their annual review and help them in their future careers. Due to the nature of the IT industry and the need for good PMs it is often very hard for a PM to find time to do formal project reviews. However, a good PM will have this time factored in! It is important that you complete a project review form for each team member and where possible meet and go through this form with them. Project reviews are a key factor in helping to improve team members' skill sets and morale.

Tip: You should also ask each team member to complete an upward review form for you, which you can hand over to your manager at the end of the project. It is a great way to learn about what skills you need to improve!

The following outlines the key areas of focus for a team member review and for each description a rating should be applied:

Project Review Areas for Team Members

Area	Description	Rating
General findings	Quality of work Consistency of work Productivity Team impact Customer impact Deliverable quality	❏ Exceeds ❏ Meets fully ❏ Meets mostly ❏ Does not meet
Core competencies (tailor per) role played on project)	Customer focus Creative problem solving Self-management Interpersonal effectiveness Teamwork Leadership Consulting skills	❏ Exceeds ❏ Meets fully ❏ Meets mostly ❏ Does not meet ❏ Exceeds

	Management skills Technology Design Business skills	❑ Meets fully ❑ Meets mostly ❑ Does not meet
General assessment	Areas of strength Areas for development Training requirements Career aspirations Additional information	❑ Exceeds ❑ Meets fully ❑ Meets mostly ❑ Does not meet

Sunset Reviews

A sunset review is a final (two to three hour) meeting that should occur upon completion of a project. Delivery team sunset reviews should occur within two weeks of project completion and customer sunset reviews within two months. The format is the same for both.

The full team should be present and an independent facilitator should facilitate the meeting. Prior to the meeting each team member should be sent a questionnaire to complete and bring to the meeting with them. This questionnaire has three simple questions:

1. What went well on the project?
2. What didn't go so well?
3. What improvements would you suggest?

The facilitator can then gather all the answers and allow an open discussion on the questionnaire responses. Following the meeting the facilitator should document everything that was said at the meeting and circulate it to all who attended. The PM should then prepare a feedback presentation and present it to a management team, who should include representatives from operations, sales, finance, HR, IT and relevant business managers. The feedback presentation will then act as a catalyst for any changes that are required for future projects.

Project Harvesting

A PM and TL should analyse carefully the following areas to harvest for future projects. An organisation that implements a lot of projects should organise an intranet repository to capture and store project tools and information that can be reused:

- ❑ Project documents, templates, checklists
- ❑ Project technologies – reusable components
- ❑ Project methodology – environment set-up, lessons learned.

Case Studies

Marketing should always want to tell the story of a good project that was completed for external customers! As PM you should always be thinking of your project as a potential case study and towards the end of a project you need to start preparing your customer for that possibility. The PM and TL will need to spend time summarising the project, the technologies used, time-frames, areas of pain and how they were resolved, the business benefits etc. Case studies are the best selling tool you can have for new business generation.

So if you have a good project you should spend time at the end helping marketing to document it!

Benefit Analysis

It is important to spend time with a customer a couple of months post project implementation to assess the impact the project has had. We would recommend that this is done before any "phase two" work commences, as it is only when the project is assessed in the real world that the project's true benefits can be seen. A lot of enhancement requests can arise during the testing phase but these enhancements should be stalled until a benefit analysis has been completed. The original business case can be used as the basis for this analysis.

It Could Happen to you ...

Every Project Has a Good Outcome!

I was working as a young GUI developer on a very long, badly scoped, badly managed, complicated government project in the US. The hours were long and the delivery team though united was exhausted. We really couldn't see what